Quilts from the Civil War

NINE PROJECTS
HISTORIC NOTES
DIARY ENTRIES

Barbara Brackman

with designs and patterns by Terry Clothier Thompson

C&T PUBLISHING

©1997 Barbara Brackman

Editor: Liz Aneloski
Technical Editor: Diana Roberts
Copy Editor: Judith Moretz
Cover Designers: Kathy Lee and John Cram
Design Director: Diane Pedersen
Book Designer: Ewa Gavrielov
Illustrator: Kandy Petersen
Photographer: Jon Blumb, unless otherwise noted

Published by C&T Publishing, Inc. P.O. Box 1456, Lafayette, California 94549

Library of Congress Cataloging-in-Publication Data

Brackman, Barbara
            Quilts from the Civil War: nine projects, historic notes, diary entries / Barbara Brackman.
                        p.   cm.
            Includes index.
            ISBN 1-57120-033-9 (pbk.)
            1. Patchwork--Patterns.   2. Quilts--United States--History--19th century
3. United States --History--Civil War, 1861-1865--Women.
I. Title.
TT835.B6423   1997
746.46 041--DC21   97-12181
                                                                                         CIP

Printed in China
10 9 8 7 6 5 4 3

Contents

Timeline

The American Civil War lasted four years, from April, 1861 to April, 1865. The conflict was the result of events throughout the first six decades of the 19th century.

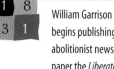 The importation of African slaves to the U.S. made illegal.

1831 William Garrison begins publishing abolitionist newspaper the *Liberator*.

 First Boston Female Anti-Slavery Fair held in December.

1838 Queen Victoria's Coronation—Britain outlaws slavery.

1844 Elias Howe patents a sewing machine with an eye at the point of the needle and an interlocking stitch.

 Texas and Florida admitted as slave states.

 Free Soil Party formed to urge prohibition of slavery into new territories.

 Isaac Singer patents an improved sewing machine, which he sells for $125.

 Harriet Beecher Stowe publishes *Uncle Tom's Cabin*.

 Kansas Territory opened for settlement. Stephen Douglas introduces the Kansas Nebraska Act, mandating that settlers decide whether state is to be free or slave.

 James Buchanan, a Southern sympathizer, elected President. Singer and his partner Edward Clark begin the installment plan by which one can purchase a sewing machine for $5 per month. They also begin selling the Turtle Back, the first machine for the home rather than the factory.

November 6 Abraham Lincoln elected President.

December 20 South Carolina secedes from the Union.

January 9 Mississippi secedes, followed by Florida, Alabama, Georgia, and Louisiana.

January 29 Kansas becomes the 34th state.

February 1 Texas secedes, making seven Confederate sisters.

February 9 Jefferson Davis elected President of the Confederate States of America.

March 4 The Stars and Bars adopted as the Confederate Flag.

April 12 Fort Sumter fired on by South Carolinians.

April 15 Lincoln calls up troops for a thirty-day war.

April 16 Confederate government asks for 32,000 troops.

April 17 Virginia secedes.

April 19 Southern ports blockaded.

April 27 Three to four thousand women meet at the Cooper Institute in New York to organize the Women's Central Association for Relief (what will become the auxiliary of the U.S. Sanitary Commision).

4

1 8 6 1

May 6
Arkansas secedes, followed on the 20th by North Carolina.

June
Peterson's Magazine publishes the first color quilt pattern for a "Stars and Stripes Bed-Quilt."

June 8
Tennessee secedes and Mary Hughes Lord appliqués a Union flag to a silk quilt she has been sewing.

June 13
Union government approves a plan for a Sanitary Commission.

July
Women North and South begin organizing Soldiers' Aid Societies.

August
First Confiscation Act declares slaves who enter Union territory as "contraband" who can be confiscated and essentially freed.

November
Union Navy captures Port Royal, South Carolina, inspiring Confederate women in New Orleans to stage a Gunboat Fair.

1 8 6 2

January 28
Christian Commission organized.

April
Confederates begin drafting men 20 to 45 years old.

May 11
The CSS Virginia is sunk to prevent her capture by Union forces.

July
Second Confiscation Act liberates slaves behind Union lines. Also enlists free blacks and freed slaves in the Army.

September 22
Lincoln publishes the Emancipation Proclamation.

1 8 6 3

Ebenezer Butterick begins making paper dress patterns.

January 1
Emancipation Proclamation becomes effective.

March
Union begins drafting men.

May 1
The Confederacy changes flag from Stars and Bars to Stainless Banner.

June 1
Robert E. Lee becomes Confederate Commander-in-Chief.

July 4
West Virginia, whose Union sympathizers broke away from Confederate Virginia, becomes the 35th star on the Union flag.

August 25
Union Army in Missouri issues General Order No. 11, evacuating four counties bordering Kansas.

October 27
Chicago's Sanitary Commission Fair, The Northwestern Fair begins.

November 19
Lincoln gives Gettysburg Address.

1 8 6 4

March 4
Grant becomes Commander-in-Chief of the Union Army.

April
New York's Great Metropolitan Fair held to raise money for the Sanitary Commission.

July 4
Nevada becomes the 36th star on the Union flag.

August
The Ladies Christian Commission of San Francisco sponsors a Grand Fair.

October 5
Mary Jones of Georgia records paying $16 dollars a yard for calico.

1 8 6 5

January 29
Fair held at the old State House in Columbia, South Carolina.

March 4
Lincoln inaugurated.

April 9
Lee surrenders to Grant at Appomatox and the War is over.

April 15
John Wilkes Booth assassinates Abraham Lincoln.

December
Thirteenth amendment abolishing slavery is ratified by 3/4 of the states.

Calico Flag by Linda Frost.
A copy of a flag made by Palmyra
Mitchell, Union Mills, Missouri, 1863. For
her story, see page 92.

Collection of period pieced items with a
reproduction "housewife" or sewing kit.

INTRODUCTION

Last year I was in Charleston, South Carolina, thinking about writing this book when someone apologized to me for the attitude I might encounter as a Yankee in the old Southern city. "Please understand," she laughed, "the 'Woah' is not over down here." I could only tell her that the "Woah" was not over in my hometown either. In Lawrence, Kansas, we had just decided, after much community discussion and dissension, to name our new school Free State High School. Students would be ever reminded of our origins back in the years of Bleeding Kansas, when free-state Jayhawkers battled slave-state Bushwhackers over the question of slavery.

This book on America's Civil War and its quilts, then, is by a Northerner, proud to live in a town with a Free State High School. I realize where my prejudices lie, yet I have tried to listen carefully to the voices of the Southern women and give them and their quilts equal weight in telling the story of the War.

I have also tried to bring these women alive with words from their diaries, letters, and memoirs, with photographs of them and their children, and especially with their quilts. In their written words I have left grammar and spelling errors as they appeared in print, but with spoken words transcribed by someone else into dialect I have paraphrased the dialect into regular English. The dialect serves to distance us too much from the speaker.

The book encourages the reader to make a connection to the women of the Civil War era by copying their quilts. Some quilters make a faithful *copy* of the original, matching each block to reproduction fabrics. These faithful copies are wonderful exercises in quilt history, teaching the copyist much about fabric and design attitudes of the era. Many quilters make an *adaptation*, beginning with the basic idea, but adding and changing borders, updating color schemes, and introducing a modern aesthetic. And some use a quilt or an incident as a point of inspiration, creating an *interpretation*—a quilt that might have existed.

Use the many letters and diaries of Civil War era women that are being published and republished today for inspiration. In their words you'll find lives that were funny, sweet and sad, and sometimes, like that described in Mary Lincoln's letters, absolutely horrific. You'll find those women staring soberly at us in the *carte-de-visite* and tintype photographs to be just like us and yet not the least like us. You'll make new friends with women who lived long ago. Nothing can give you better insight into the era.

And while we are on the subject of new friends and old, I want to thank those who made the quilts pictured in the book. I owe much to Terry Clothier Thompson, whose fanciful interpretations inspire so many others. Terry wrote much of the pattern directions here. And thanks to Cherie Ralston, who checked our patterns and made a wonderful Union quilt. I also want to thank quiltmakers Gail Bakkom, Bobbi Finley, Linda Frost, Nancy Hornback, Mary Madden, Patti Mersmann, Ruth Powers, Sherri Rush, Wava Stoker-Musgrave, Shirley Wedd, Shirlene Wedd, and Jeananne Wright.

CHAPTER I

"Petticoat Plotters" Quilts for Freedom's Fair

"To the chivalrous sons of the South:

Most chivalrous gentlemen—pardon us; pray

And pity our present condition.

The lady fanatics have carried the day,

And openly preach Abolition!

The petticoat plotters, with might and with main,

Are tearing the bonds of the Union atwain."

Ladies' Anti-Slavery Society of [Concord] New Hampshire,
Liberator, January 3, 1835

Unknown woman with needlework.

Abolition:
The idea of eliminating slavery.
Emancipation:
The Presidential decree that liberated slaves in Confederate territory in 1863.
Thirteenth Amendment:
The amendment to the U.S. Constitution, passed in 1865, stating that slavery shall not exist within the United States.

More ink and paper has been devoted to the American Civil War than to any other topic in the English language. Yet the shelves and shelves of books rarely discuss the War from the perspective of half of those who lived through it—the women. And too often when women are discussed they are portrayed as sitting mute, impotently waiting at home. In truth, women played many active roles in the Civil War, roles that are hardly remembered. Among their most vigorous activities was chafing the nation's conscience in the thirty years leading up to the conflict.

Abolition, the elimination of slavery, began as a radical idea held by a few religious and political Americans. Through the first half of the nineteenth century abolition grew into a national concept that resulted in Emancipation, and later the Thirteenth amendment to the Constitution, which freed the slaves, in 1865. Many white Americans initially resisted the idea of absolute freedom for all African-Americans, but they also realized the hypocrisy of a system of slavery thriving in a nation rooted in liberty.

Abolitionists forced this disparity into the center of a national debate about American identity. Using tactics familiar today they relied on the written word to raise consciousness about the evils of slavery. Abolitionists presented their arguments in newspapers, petitions, fiction, political pamphlets and tracts, broadsides (handbills), and even in needlework. "When pincushions are periodicals and needlebooks are tracts, discussion can hardly be stifled or slavery perpetuated."[1]

At the heart of their message was a conviction that slaves were people with human needs and human rights, a radical idea because, in the words of Angelina Grimké Weld, "One who is a slaveholder at heart never recognizes a human being in a slave."

Fragment of a tied comforter made in Boston about 1855, with a photograph of Dr. Sylvester B. Prentiss. Collection of the Kansas State Historical Society. Photo courtesy of the Kansas Quilt Project.

The family story that has been handed down with this quilt indicates it was made by the women of the Boston Emigrant Aid Society to be sold at a charity raffle in Lawrence, Kansas, in 1855. The wool circles behind the ties were said to be cut from Revolutionary War uniforms. The comforter raised money to feed New Englanders settling Kansas in the hopes that their votes would make the Territory free soil rather than slave. The quilt was bought by Dr. Sylvester B. Prentiss, who impressed upon his family its value. At some point it was cut into several pieces, probably so that each child could have a souvenir. The museum owns two pieces.

Boston was a hotbed of abolition, the home of the fight against the national complacency. Chief among the Boston newspapers preaching abolition was *Liberator*, published from 1831 to 1866. Back pages of the paper invited the reader into the small world of Boston radicals. *Liberator* carried announcements of meetings and social events, advertisements for goods produced by free labor rather than slave, want ads for ex-slaves looking for rooms, and letters arguing fine points of the cause. Editor William Lloyd Garrison was an extremist whose editorial passion for freedom extended to women. Sarah Grimké, who wrote a column on women's rights, was one of several women correspondents.

Women were important in the pages of *Liberator* because they were important in the movement, earning a reputation as political fanatics with their speeches and writings about the cause and their petitions to Congress. In their anti-slavery societies, which met separately from the men's, fund-raising was a primary activity. The major annual event was a Fair, much like the Christmas crafts bazaars church groups hold today. Women and children donated handmade items to be sold to benefit the abolitionists' work. Booths featured craft items and gifts, a refreshment area, a post office offering letters and cards with hand-lettered missives and mottoes, and a bookshop selling abolitionist literature. "Many an individual who never would have read an anti-slavery publication or entered a lecture room, has been induced by curiosity, or the demands of the Christmas or New Year's Holiday to visit this annual scene of Abolition business and has left with a juster appreciation of [our] motives," wrote the correspondent for *Liberator*.[2]

Those unable to create original mottoes for their implements of housewifery need look no further than pages of *Liberator*. The weekly "Literary, Miscellaneous and Moral" page featured poetry about the plight of the slaves. A. R. P. Danvers's verses may lack soaring imagery, but they would fit nicely on a gentleman's handkerchief:

> *". . . I'd sooner spend my days within*
> *Some dark and dismal cave*
> *Than to be guilty of the sin*
> *Of holding one poor slave."*[3]

Detail of an album quilt by Barbara Brackman, Lawrence, Kansas, 1996 with an antique block on top of it.

H. H. Coursen's friendship block dates from between 1840 and 1865, and features the tiny cross-stitch embroidery that girls were taught in school until technological marvels such as indelible ink for fabric and the sewing machine made such handwork obsolete. The reproduction fabrics in the fanciful quilt top under the old block are copies of the Turkey red prints that were so popular in the decades before the Civil War. The originals were imported from France, printed in Provence. Look for red backgrounds with figures in yellow, blue, green, and black (or a very dark brown). Cone shapes, what we call paisleys, are good reproductions, as are *mignonettes*, the little florals that are isolated from each other. These French provincial designs are not easy to find, but the reds give an authentic air to any copy of a mid-nineteenth-century quilt.

Free-State Album Quilt by Mary Wilk Madden, Topeka, Kansas, 1996

Mary's interpretation of a Civil-War era album quilt might be the kind of quilt that was inked with "mottoes and devices. . . . weapons for Abolitionists." The pattern for this type of album was pictured in the March, 1860, issue of *Godey's Lady's Book*, with no name given. It's the pattern used by Caroline Richards and her sewing group in Canandaigua, New York, for their friendship quilts made during and shortly after the War. In the block centers they inked Union sentiments as well as comments about their friendship and the marriages the quilts commemorated.

Mary has pieced 56 blocks in reproduction calicoes for our imaginary quilt that might have been made in Kansas in the 1850s. We inked the names of men and women who worked to make the Kansas Territory a free state rather than a slave state. The names include martyrs such as Charles W. Dow who was the first person killed in the Kansas Troubles. We included some of our heroes like Clarina I. H. Nichols and Hannah Anderson Ropes, feminists who came to Kansas for the free-state cause.

Civil War re-enactors might want to make blocks in the field and ask fellow re-enactors to sign the patches, inking a record of new and old friends.

Detail of an album quilt by Mary Wilk Madden, Topeka, Kansas, 1996

Clarina Nichols, Jane Carruth, Sara Robinson, and Miriam Davis Colt went to Kansas to add their voices to the free state movement. This fanciful album quilt is the kind they might have signed in the late 1850s.

Swatches and blocks of bright blue show how popular Prussian blue cottons were in the 1840-1865 era. The dye is natural, a mineral dye that was easily printed with browns. The buff and blue stripes, plaids, and florals were popular for quilts and women's dresses right before the War. Notice the rainbow blues in which the color washes from dark to bright. Look for vivid blues, especially blue rainbow prints, for reproduction quilts.

Detail of *Abolition Crib Quilt* by Barbara Brackman, Lawrence, Kansas, 1996

The original from which this quilt was adapted was sold at a Fair in 1836. It is now in the collection of the Society for the Preservation of New England Antiquities. Reproductions of Turkey reds and Prussian blue prints give the new quilt an antique look. The poem reads as follows:

Mother! When around your child
You clasp your arm in love,
And when with grateful joy you raise
Your eyes to God above—
Think of the Negro-mother,
When her child is torn away—
Sold for a little slave—oh then,
For that poor mother pray!"

Abolition Crib Quilt by Barbara Brackman, Lawrence, Kansas, 1996

In 1836, the women of Boston put on an Anti-Slavery Fair. One cradle quilt made for that fair caught the eye of the correspondent for *Liberator*, the abolitionist newspaper, who described it as "made of patchwork in small stars; and on the central star was written with indelible ink [a poem]." The very same quilt is in the collection of Boston's Society for the Preservation of New England Antiquities.[4]

The pattern is a star known by various names today, such as Evening Star, Sawtooth Star, or Variable Star. The original is 45˝ x 37˝, with 63 five-inch blocks arranged side-by-side in a 7 by 9 block set. It has no border but is bound with a pink and white calico print. The maker arranged the blocks by color; the central block with the poem inscribed had a light print center; the rest were varieties of pinks, browns, blue gingham checks, and two bright Turkey red blocks in the center area.

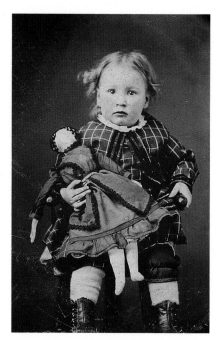

This child's curls, doll, and skirt say "little girl" to us, but the portrait is probably a boy wearing pants under his skirt. The doll's hair is of printed fabric.

Surviving quilts also testify to the link between quilts and abolition. Pennsylvania's Lycoming County Historical Society owns a pair of long, narrow signature quilts, once joined as a single piece. The Turkey red album blocks feature over one hundred names, many Chester County Quakers, a few of whom inked verses about abolition. Such a quilt may have been sold at the Philadelphia Anti-Slavery Fairs that began in 1836. The Chester County Historical Society owns a baby quilt by the Herrick Sewing Circle of Lancaster County, Pennsylvania. Eight blocks in the album pattern frame a central feathered star inked with a poem that summarizes the quilt's origins in the anti-slavery cause:

> "Do thou, sweet babe, in safety sleep
> Beneath this canopy so fair.
> Formed thy fragile limbs to keep
> Protected from the chilling air.
> Formed in love for Freedom's Fair
> To aid a righteous cause
> To help its advocates declare
> God's unchangeable and equal laws."[5]

Liberator
Boston
January 2, 1837
The Ladies' Fair
The proposed Anti-Slavery Fair was held on Thursday, the 22nd of December. The convenient and well-lighted hall called the Artist's Gallery was duly prepared for our reception, and we had not the slightest reason to complain of reluctance or want of courtesy on the part of the proprietor. The Hall was filled with visitors at an early hour, and continued full until late in the evening. Very many of these were not abolitionists but belonged to a large and increasing class of the community which has been strongly abolitionized by Anti-Slavery efforts. Not a few of the wives and daughters of "gentlemen of property and standing" were among the purchasers.

The cake-table was loaded with varieties of cake made of sugar not manufactured by slaves, and near was placed the motto, Free Labor. There was a great variety in the articles, and many of them were very handsome and tasteful. The ladies have ever regarded the pecuniary benefit derived but one of several reasons in their favor. The main object is to keep the subject before the public eye, and by every innocent expedient to promote perpetual discussion.

To promote this favorite object, various mottoes and devices were stamped upon the articles offered for sale. Bunches of quilts bore the label, "Twenty-five Weapons for Abolitionists." On one side of the pen-wipers was inscribed, "Wipe out the blot of Slavery"; on the other, "Plead the cause with thy Pen." On some needle-books was printed, "May the use of our needles prick the consciences of slaveholders"; others were made in the form of small shoes, and on the soles was written, "Trample not on the Oppressed." Some watch-cases bore the inscription, "The political economist counts time by *years*, the suffering slave reckons it by *minutes*"; on others was written, "The greatest friend of Tuth is *Time*; her greatest enemy is *Prejudice*." Small hearts cut from a knot of white oak were called, "Hearts of Oak for Abolitionists."

"There was a small "Thermometer of the Heart," fastened upon a pillar of white sugar. The glass tube was filled with rose-colored spirits of wine, which rose with the warmth of the hand. The scale from freezing point upward was thus graduated.

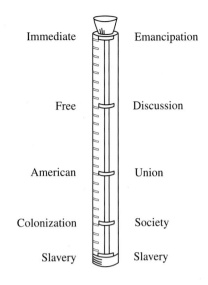

Immediate — Emancipation

Free — Discussion

American — Union

Colonization — Society

Slavery — Slavery

CHAPTER 2

"Emancipation Without Proclamation" Quilts and the Underground Railroad

Away to the land of the North!—for her star

Shall beacon thy course from its blue home afar—

W. H. Burleigh in *Liberator*, December 9, 1837

Log Cabin in the Streak of Lightning Set by Charlotte Varnum Cutter (1803-1880), made 1860-1880 in Vinland, Douglas County, Kansas. Collection of Watkins Community Museum of History, Lawrence, Kansas

Charlotte Cutter was a New Englander, a widow who immigrated to the Kansas Territory with her three children in 1859. Her Log Cabin quilt is made of the light wool printed fabrics so popular for women's and girls' clothing during the Civil War era. She may have chosen the pattern for political reasons; as a New Englander in Kansas she was likely a Republican and Unionist who'd have voted for Lincoln if she could. Or it may be that she never gave a thought to the political symbolism and was merely caught up in the fashion for these quilts that raged in the 1870s.

The belief that quilts were used as signals on the Underground Railroad is certainly one of the strongest chords of historic symbolism ringing through today's quilt stories. People who take my classes in dating and identifying antique quilts often tell the story of the Log Cabin quilt and its role in the secret network of "stations" that assisted slaves on their escapes. Log Cabin quilts, they tell me, hung on laundry lines to indicate safe havens for African-Americans running north. These particular Log Cabin quilts, the story goes, can be identified by black center squares, a contrast to the more common block with red centers. Other tales tell of quilts as symbolic maps for the northern journey and patterns encoded with information about way stations. Art historian Raymond G. Dobard has woven together the threads of current discussion about the role of quilts in the Underground Railroad. In "Coded in Cloth: The Visible and Tangible in African-American Quilts," he refers to the use of specific patterns, particularly Jacob's Ladder or the Underground Railroad design, as signals. Noting the connection to the song *Jacob's Ladder*, also seen as a coded message, he concludes, "I strongly believe that the singing of certain spirituals along with the display of specific patterns constituted coded instructions."[6]

As a European-American, I live outside the community that has transmitted oral traditions of life under slavery. Yet as a historian I have read many primary and secondary documents about slavery, especially the published letters and memoirs written by persons of African-American descent and narratives transcribed from their testimony. As a quilt historian I know much about quilts made before 1865 and those made by succeeding generations of Americans. Fabrics, styles, and techniques changed significantly in the 1860s, enabling one to discriminate between pre-War and post-War quilts. Too many popular authors and some academicians writing about the historical role of quilts have not acquired a knowledge of dating and thus draw conclusions based on misdated quilts. They rely upon family traditions and museum records, which can be quite imprecise. Unfortunately, too many conclusions about Civil War traditions are based on misdated quilts.

My knowledge of pre-Civil War quilts and my reading about personal experiences in the era lead me to question today's conventional wisdom about the role of quilts on the Underground Railroad. These assumptions include the ideas that:

1. Quilts were used as signals on the Underground Railroad to indicate a safe house;
2. Log Cabin quilts with black centers were favored as signals;
3. Patterns such as Underground Railroad contained coded maps to lead one north.

Most Americans are familiar with the Underground Railroad as a clandestine road to freedom for African-Americans fleeing slavery. As a history educator, I hear misconceptions about the form the road took

Maria Weems escaping in male attire, from William Still's 1872 book *The Underground Railroad*

Birds in the Air. Detail of a copy of an abolitionist quilt by Patti Mersmann, Lawrence, Kansas, 1996

Patti's cotton copy of a silk quilt features a drawing of a shackled slave like the original, which is still in the family of the maker. The image was important in the abolitionist movement, appearing on objects from needlecases to china. Southerner Ella Clanton Thomas wrote in disgust that she had heard that abolitionist Gerrit Smith asked his guests to eat from plates decorated with chained slaves. For a photograph and instructions for this quilt see the project instructions beginning on page 25 and Inking on page 125.

15

and how common it was. One error identifies the railroad literally as a road that ran underground—if not a road of rails, engines, and passenger cars, then as a series of tunnels. Below-ground structures from Kansas cisterns to Thomas Jefferson's underground walkway at Monticello have been romanticized as fragments of the Underground Railroad.

Such misconceptions are due, in part, to the extended metaphor that abolitionists developed in the pre- and post-Civil War years when railroads were new and fascinating. People associated with the roads to freedom freely used terms associated with the concept of a literal Underground Railroad. The press and the public called runaways "packages," "merchandise," and "goods." Information about how to make contact was a "ticket." Those who assisted were "stationmasters," "engineers," and "conductors." The line had a self-styled President, Levi Coffin. Places to sleep or to get a meal and clean clothing were "stations." But the concept of a railroad was pure metaphor, having little to do with the practicalities of the escapes.

Rachel Bowman Cormany was a young schoolteacher in 1860, boarding around with parents of the students near Worthington, Ohio, as teachers at the time often did. One of the families was that of Ezra Gardner. Rachel wrote in her diary:

"June 21, 1860 . . . At dusk Mr Gardner got a note from Worthington telling him that a fugitive slave was there ready to be expressed on the underground road. . . . It was 4 Oclock this morning before we got started, but still got to Worthington and got the girl (who looks as though she was about 18 years old & quite smart) before many folks were astir & got back to Mr Potters before six Oclock. . . . As soon as breakfast was over and the horse could be gotten out, he was taken to Mrs. Potters and Mrs P and little daughter with the fugitive got in the covered buggy. When they came to Old uncle Ozems [Ozen Gardner], as the neighbors call him, they stopped. we all went out to see them, she had no gloves & it was a little dangerous of being detected without, so I gave her mine."[7]

Rachel's little gift, a pair of gloves to help the girl look like a lady, tells us how important clothing was for escapees. Slaves often wore simple clothes of heavy cotton, called Osnaburg or slave-cloth. Women wore turbans, aprons, and heavy shoes, which branded them as slaves as clearly as stripes marked a prisoner. Escapees wishing to pass as white or as free people of color must dress as ladies with bonnets, street dresses, and gloves. Supplying runners with clothing was part of the work of the anti-slavery societies. Levi Coffin, in his *Reminiscences*, told of women's work in the underground in Cincinnati. "When it was known by some of the prominent ladies of the village that a large company of fugitives were in the neighborhood, they met together to prepare some clothing for them."[8]

Detail of *Union Star* by Terry Clothier Thompson, Lawrence, Kansas, 1996. Full quilt pictured on page 33.

Call to Kansas by Ruth Powers, Carbondale, Kansas, 1996

Inspired by lines of poetry, Ruth Powers designed a fanciful quilt that combines nineteenth-century color and pattern with a contemporary sensibility. North Stars light the path out of the darkness of slavery. The floral border symbolizes the lines by abolitionist Lucy Larcom who encouraged free-state sympathizers to crusade against Southern immigrants to Kansas. Her "Call to Kansas" invited "Sister true, join us too, where the Kansas flows; Let the Northern lily bloom with the Southern rose." For another quilt inspired by these lines see page 70.

Few things are more American than a search for freedom. Since quilts also enjoy an important role in American myth, their role as signals to escapees to freedom is no surprise.

How could a runaway know who was friendly to "Emancipation without Proclamation" as one Underground Railroad conductor, Clarina Nichols, called it? Few tales of signals appear in print and no first-hand accounts by African-Americans reveal any mention of quilts as devices to indicate safety, danger, or recognition. However, we may argue that a lack of published information about Underground Railroad signals is no proof that signals did not exist. Secret signals are, by definition, not to be published or spoken of. A Jewish friend retracing the steps that his French mother took to escape the Nazis reminds me that even today, those who took that underground road will not reveal their secrets because they fear such persecution might happen again. [9]

Although there were probably many signals for personal and place recognition, and it may be possible that quilts did mark safe houses in the ante-bellum United States, the Log Cabin pattern could not be the quilt that hung on the line. Log Cabin quilts, so called because they are pieced of fabric strips built up like logs, were most popular between 1870 and 1920, with the earliest published example inscribed 1869. Quilt historian Virginia Gunn has found three written references to Log Cabin quilts as fundraisers for the Union cause in 1863, the likely year for the beginning of the style. At that point the Underground Railroad no longer functioned as it had before the War. The need for secrecy and coded messages in the border states passed as slaves' status changed with their legal descriptions. [10]

Clarina I. Howard Nichols in New England before she came to Kansas to help on the Underground Railroad. Courtesy of the Kansas State Historical Society.

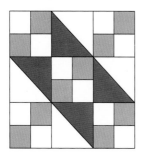

Ruth Finley's depiction of the Underground Railroad pattern; one we never see in quilts made during the days of the Underground Railroad.

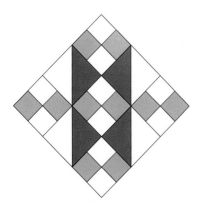

Finley's block placed on point resembles a typical set for four-patch blocks in the mid-nineteenth century.

Kind of four-patch strip quilt that might have been called Underground Railroad in the mid-nineteenth century. Finley's vision of the repeat is difficult to find but it is in here.

So, we must not imagine Log Cabin quilts as signals in the decades before the War. Rather, like Emancipation, the pattern grew out of the War. It is more historically accurate to view their symbolic function as an indicator of allegiance to President Abraham Lincoln (our second Log Cabin president) and the Union cause. After Lincoln's death in 1865 Log Cabin quilts might have become a memorial to the martyred president. One indication that a Union connection continued is the relative lack of late nineteenth-century Log Cabin quilts made in the former Confederate states.

Were quilts used as coded maps? The patchwork pattern Underground Railroad might be seen as such a device, but again there are no surviving quilts in the design from the era of slavery. Underground Railroad is an arrangement of squares and triangles forming a diagonal trail across both the block and the quilt top. In her 1929 book, *Old Patchwork Quilts and the Women Who Made Them*, pattern historian Ruth Finley used the design to illustrate the variety in names, shading, and patterns. For this one block she listed names such as Jacob's Ladder, Stepping Stones, The Tail of Benjamin's Kite, The Trail of the Covered Wagon, Wagon Tracks, and The Underground Railroad. Finley was specific about the regional origins of the name, telling us that Underground Railroad was used in the Western Reserve, the northeastern area of Ohio where she was raised. She also mentioned how the names evolved over time and locale, noting that Jacob's Ladder was of "shadowy pre-Revolutionary origin," and that Underground Railroad "flashed pictures of Eliza of *Uncle Tom's Cabin* crossing the ice from Kentucky to Ohio whence the underground railroad carried runaway slaves to the promised land of Canada."[11]

Perhaps Finley knew a block pieced of squares and triangles as Underground Railroad, but surviving quilts containing her design date only to the turn of the last century, so it is unlikely that diagonal quilt patterns in this nine-patch design were used as symbolic maps to freedom. As with the stories about the Log Cabin, the major evidence is a missing quilt. I've seen no quilts in Finley's pattern made before the Civil War.

There are two possible answers to the mystery of the missing Underground Railroad quilts:

The first is that the pattern developed thirty or forty years after the end of slavery. In the last quarter of the nineteenth century, when the history of the Underground Railroad and personal reminiscences of the War were being published, a relatively new pattern may have been named after the Underground Railroad. Finley's pattern should then be viewed as a commemorative design.

Four Patch in a Strip Set, maker unknown, 1860-1870, Collection of Kimberly Wulfert

This crib quilt is typical of mid-century utility quilts in its simple pattern and scrappy nature. The strip set was popular through the first half of the nineteenth century, but rather uncommon after the War. The little quilt contains a treasure, a Civil War commemorative fabric. Can this quilt also be a clue to the mystery of the Underground Railroad design? Is the elusive pattern just a four-patch set on point in strip fashion? See a detail of the commemorative print on page 30.

A second possibility is that Finley combined in a single nine-patch both block and setting triangles for an old-fashioned version of a common four-patch. Quilts with four-patches set on point in strips of triangles were popular in the years before the Civil War. These rows of four-patches might have symbolized a journey, a trip on the Underground Railroad. When Finley drafted the pattern, she made significant changes to a design that made it unrecognizable. Could it be that the Underground Railroad quilts of the mid-nineteenth century have been hiding, like so many of the escaped slaves, in plain sight?

Readers may choose to believe either story, but in both cases we cannot imagine these quilts used as maps. Rather they are symbolic designs, honoring the underground and the brave people who rode it, people who were in the words of conductor William Still, ". . . ignorant of the distance they had to travel, and the dangers and sufferings to be endured. But they 'trusted in God' and kept the North Star in view."[12]

$20 REWARD!!

Runaway or Stolen,

from the Subscriber, on the 27th of last month, a negro woman and two children; the woman is tall and black, and a few days before she went off, I burnt her with a hot iron on the left side of her face; I tried to make the letter M, and she kept a cloth over her head and face and a fly bonnet on her head, so as to cover the burn, she has a very wide vacancy between her upper fore teeth, her children are both boys; the oldest one is in his seventh year; he is a mulatto; he has blue eyes; the youngest is black; he is in his fifth year, he is cockeyed, inclined to be cross-eyed. The woman's name is Bettey, commonly called Bet. The oldest boy's name is Burrel and the other ones name is Gray. The above reward of twenty dollars will be given to any person that will deliver the said negroes to me. It is probable they may attempt to pass as free.

Micajah Ricks
Nash County July 7, 1838

Underground Railroad

Underground Railroad by Terry Clothier
Thompson, Lawrence, Kansas, 1996

Inspired by stories about the Underground Railroad of the 1840s and 1850s, Terry Clothier Thompson designed a fanciful quilt interpreting the road out of slavery. She used reproduction prints and a sensibility that echoes the quilts of the era, with a strip set and four-patches on point. The golden stars sparkling in the dark blue strips light the path to freedom. Variations of these nine-patch stars have many names, and here she calls it a North Star.

Size: 64⅝″ x 76″
Blocks: Four-Patches, 4″ finished; North Stars, 5⅝″ finished

FABRIC REQUIREMENTS

- Four-Patch Blocks: Fabric to total 1 yard. You will need 50 four-patch blocks. Collect a large variety of cotton prints to achieve a scrap look in the quilt. A contrast of light and dark make the four-patch more interesting, but these days we are sometimes surprised by the mid-nineteenth-century attitude towards contrast; they often pieced dark to dark.
- North Stars and Setting Triangles: ¼ yard of solid gold and 1¼ yards of solid blue
- Setting Strips: The setting strips of the time would be a large-scale chintz or stripe: 4 yards
- Backing: 4 yards
- Binding: ½ yard (See Binding page 123.)

CUTTING AND SEWING

Four-Patches

This fast cutting and piecing method is perfect for four-patches. Cut 2½″ strips and stitch a light and a dark strip together with a ¼″ seam allowance. Press seams to the darkest side. Cut 2½″ units from the strips. Stitch two of the units together, rotating so the darks and lights are opposite. If you haven't tried laundry line piecing (chain piecing), where you never lift your presser foot, this is the perfect place to try it. Stitch the first four-patch together on the machine, and when you come to the end of the seam, do not lift the presser foot or needle. Just add a second four-patch behind the first and continue stitching, leaving about a ½″ of thread between each block. This chain piecing technique saves time because you don't have to cut the threads and adjust the needle. This is my favorite way to machine piece. When you've sewn all your four-patches together you can snip the threads that connect each block to the next and press. Make 50 four-patch blocks.

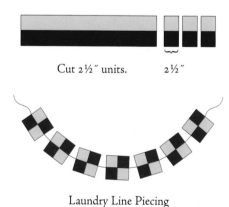

Cut 2½″ units.   2½″

Laundry Line Piecing

Setting Triangles

Cut five 6⅞″ strips, then cut thirty 6⅞″ squares. Cut the squares along both diagonals. This yields 120 setting triangles. Cutting this way assures that the straight grain of the triangles lines up with the straight grain of the setting strips and, thus, the edge of the quilt. Place the four-patches on point with the dark squares on the sides. Stitch each four-patch to a pair of blue dark triangles as shown. Stitch five strips of ten blocks each. Finish each strip by adding a pair of triangles to the ends. See the illustration at right.

North Star Blocks

Piece five North Star blocks using templates A, B, and C (page 24). Stitch a North Star block at the top of each strip of four patches.

Inking

A poem is inked in the central square of the central star. See pages 14 and 125. (Away to the land...)

Chintz Setting Strips

Measure the length of your four-patch and star strips (they should be approximately 68″). Cut the six setting strips 68″ (or your measurement) x 6½″. Stitch the pieced strips to the chintz strips.

Even with care, the strips can sometimes turn out different lengths. Don't rip out. You can deal with this problem in a true nineteenth-century fashion. Measure all your strips. Then cut the long ones to match the shorter ones. Don't cringe. It's an old-fashioned thing to do. If you just can't cut up your hard work, you can lengthen the short strips by adding a rectangle of the solid blue to the bottom end of each strip so that all the strips are the same length. No one will notice that little extra coping strip next to the bottom border.

Cutting Setting Triangles

Strip Construction

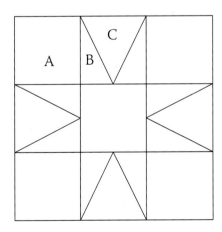

North Star Block

Top and Bottom Borders

Measure the width of your top horizontally through the middle. It should measure 64⅝″. Cut two strips 64⅝″ (or your measurement) x 6½″; or vary the width as Terry did. Add the top and bottom borders.

For tips on batting, utility quilting, and binding see the General Instructions beginning page 122.

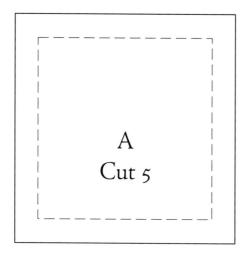

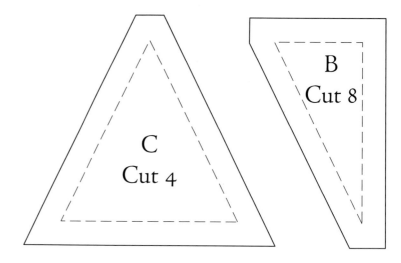

Templates

Tip: You can set lots of simple stars and blocks on point, strip fashion, and get a wonderful period look.

Quilt Top Construction

Birds in the Air

Birds in the Air by Patti Mersmann,
Lawrence, Kansas, 1996

Deborah Coates was the wife of a Quaker abolitionist who was president of the American Anti-Slavery Association in the 1830s. Her silk quilt may have been made for an Anti-Slavery Fair or merely to express her sentiments on the slavery question. In the center, a piece of fabric features the image of a bound slave with the words "Deliver me from the Oppression of Man." The quilt was so important to the family that the granddaughters of the maker cut the original in half, so each could inherit a piece. The original is 89″ x 96″ with well over one hundred blocks placed on point. The pattern is one of a variety of Sawtooth designs popular in the 1840-1865 era. Ruth Finley in her 1929 book *Old Patchwork Quilts and the Women Who Made Them* called it Birds In the Air, the perfect name for a quilt about freedom and slavery. Patti Mersmann has adapted Deborah Coates's quilt to a wall-size version in cottons.

Size: 49″ x 59½″
Blocks: 7½″ finished

FABRIC REQUIREMENTS

- Bird in the Air Blocks: The blocks are a scrap bag of reproduction fabrics with a good contrast of browns and light shirting prints. The original silk quilt featured a lot of yellow, so Patti included some yellow cottons for a little zip. Total yardage for the dark is 1¼ yards and ⅞ yard for the light; or buy a good variety of fat quarters for the 32 blocks.
- Setting triangles: ¾ yard
- Border: 1¾ yards for unpieced borders, or ⅝ yard for pieced borders
- Backing: 3 yards
- Binding: ½ yard (See Binding page 123.)

CUTTING AND SEWING
Birds in the Air Blocks
For each block you'll need three dark triangles, six light triangles, and one large dark triangle. For one block cut a 3⅜″ x 7″ strip from the dark fabric for the "birds." Cut two 3⅜″ squares and cut each square in half diagonally. Cut a 3⅜″ x 11″ strip from the light fabric. Cut three 3⅜″ squares and cut each square in half diagonally. Cut one 8⅜″ square from the dark fabric, then cut in half diagonally. Consider combining your leftovers to form blocks as Patti did.

After inking, make 32 blocks following the piecing order in the illustration. Be careful not to stretch bias edges.

Inking
Ink one light triangle with the figure and motto. (See Inking page 125.)

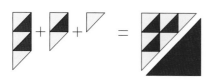

Piecing Order

Setting Triangles

Cut four 11⅞″ squares, then cut the squares along both diagonals for a total of fourteen setting triangles. The four corner triangles are cut from two 8⅜″ squares, cut in half diagonally. The straight of grain will be on the outside edges of the quilt top. Follow the illustration below to stitch the diagonal rows together.

Borders

The borders are 3″ wide finished. Measure the width of your quilt horizontally through the middle. It should measure 43″ wide. Cut two strips 43″ (or your measurement) x 3½″ for the top and bottom borders of the quilt. Add the top and bottom borders. Then measure the length of the quilt vertically through the middle. It should measure 59½″ long. Cut two side borders 59½″(or your measurement) x 3½″. Add the side borders.

For tips on batting, utility quilting, and binding see the General Instructions beginning on page 122.

Block and Corner Triangles

Setting Triangles

Quilt Top Construction

CHAPTER 3

"Rally Round the Flag, Boys!" Union and Secession Quilts

"The spirit of patriotism did not fail. The girls wore the shields of the Union on their bosoms and the skirts of their dresses was the flag of the free. It wouldn't be a pretty dress to-day but it looked glorious then, for it had meaning."

W. D. McKinistry in the *Dunkirk Journal*, 1894[13]

Union Flag by Cherie Ralston, Lawrence, Kansas, 1996

During the 1850s the topic of slavery became ever more volatile. Southerners, angered and terrified by abolitionist threats, viewed John Brown's 1859 attempt to arm a slave insurrection in Harper's Ferry, Virginia, as proof of the North's future plans. Many Southerners interpreted the Union as a Confederation, a group of states that each had a right to secede, and South Carolina, in particular, often threatened to do so. Westward expansion raised inflammatory questions about whether new territories and states would be slave or free. In the Kansas Territory free-soil and pro-slavery advocates murdered one another over the question. The conflict came to a head in the presidential election of 1860 when voters could cast their ballot for one of four candidates. John Bell represented the Constitutional Union party, an ineffective group of former Whigs. The Democrats split, offering Southern sympathizer John Breckenridge or Stephen A. Douglas, the candidate of compromise. Abraham Lincoln, representing the new Republican party, ran on a free-soil platform advocating the admission of Kansas as a free state, the 34th star on the Union flag. The least known of the candidates, Lincoln ran on a platform calling for the preservation of the Union at all costs.

Portraits of Abe and Mary Todd Lincoln by Sharon Durken Rush, Glencoe, Minnesota, 1996

Women may have had no vote, but they had opinions. Young Eliza Horton of Mobile, Alabama, wrote her cousins in Boston, "One question if you please. Is your father for Douglas? I say, 'Douglas for ever.'"

Mississippian Sarah E. Watkins wrote her daughter in Texas,

"Your Pa says if he thought you were in favor of Lincoln, he would not let you come in his house. I hope Lincoln will not be elected. The democrats are very much concerned about it. . . . I think the north and south will just keep growling at each other like cats and dogs and that is all that will be done."[14]

29

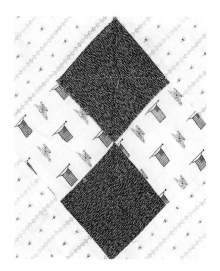

Detail of a Four Patch, maker unknown, 1860-1870, Collection of Kimberly Wulfert

The flag and cannon fabric is a conversation or object print, names used by fabric designers for realistic prints other than florals. It is one of only three conversation prints commemorating the Union cause that I have seen. Another is a brown figure, an oval surrounded by a dozen stars with the word Union in the center. It is highly unlikely that any Confederate calicoes were printed, because the calico factories were all in the North. Full quilt is pictured on page 19.

Six weeks after Lincoln's November 6, 1860, victory, South Carolina made good on her threat to secede from the Union. The independent new country believed, as Sarah Watkins did, that Lincoln would never use force to keep the Union whole. Southerners assured each other that "A lady's thimble will hold all the blood that will be shed. The Yankee traders . . . will never fight." However, if war came, South Carolina's honor demanded a fight. Ada Bacot, like so many South Carolina women, shared that sense of honor in her diary: "My fears are constantly kept alive, that S. C. will not stand her ground." [15]

Throughout the winter months South Carolina's secessionist leaders, the hotheads, persuaded other slave states to follow. An Englishman visiting Charleston in December noted the image of seven stars representing an expected confederation, an image that evolved into the first Confederate flag with a circle of seven stars on three wide red and white stripes, the "Stars and Bars." By February the seven sisters, South Carolina, Mississippi, Florida, Alabama, Georgia, Louisiana, and Texas joined in the Confederate States of America, with Jefferson Davis as President. Virginia, Arkansas, North Carolina, and Tennessee seceded as the spring changed into the first summer of war. [16]

Secession Quilt by Terry Clothier Thompson and Frankie Lister, Lawrence, Kansas, 1996

Inspired by Confederate quilts, Terry designed a quilt top to honor the patriotism of Southern women. In the center a pelican vanquishes an eagle, an image she drew from a Texas quilt made during the War by Susan Robb. Robb must have intended the pelican to symbolize the Confederacy as the eagle does the Union. In the victorious bird's mouth is a banner inked with the word "Secession." The wreath of cut-out chintz was appliquéd by Frankie to recall the *Broderie Perse* style popular before the War. In the corners Terry has pieced a traditional pattern called Seven Sisters to represent the first Confederate flag with its ring of seven stars in a field of blue.

While South Carolina led a move for secession, Confederate cannons fired the first shot, turning away a Union steamship, the *Star of the West*, trying to claim Fort Sumter in Charleston's harbor. In April, 1861, after months on a seemingly irreversible path, the Union declared War. A wave of patriotic feeling swept over the Northern states.

Stars and Stripes Quilt by Mary Rockhold-Teter of Noblesville, Indiana, 86″ x 87″, 1861. Collection of the Smithsonian Institution.

Detail of a Union quilt by Elizabeth Moffitt Lyle, Kewanee, Illinois, 1860-1864. Collection of the Smoky Hill Museum, Salina, Kansas. Photo courtesy of the Kansas Quilt Project. For a photograph and instructions for an adaptation of this quilt see the project instructions beginning on page 44.

Women expressed Union fervor in red, white, and blue Union quilts. In June, 1861, *Peterson's Magazine* published a color sketch of the "Stars and Stripes Bed-Quilt" with 34 stars representing the irrevocable Union of 34 states. Several quilters looked to *Peterson's* pattern for inspiration, while others worked out their own designs. Elizabeth Moffitt Lyle of Kewanee, Illinois, stitched a star design and in the center appliquéd a floral wreath with the words "The Constitution and Union Forever." Clara D. Moore of Rural Retsed (sic) Ohio added similar sentiments to an album quilt with the words "Constitution and Union. One and Inseperable now and forever." Federal shields adorn many of the albums made throughout the war and federal eagles flew in blocks, borders, and quilting.[17]

The best documented group of Union quilts are those made by the friends of Caroline Cowles Richards of Canandaigua, New York. Carrie discussed her quiltmaking activities in her diary, and several of the quilts she described survive in museum collections, documented by quilt historian Jacqueline Marx Atkins in her book *Shared Threads: Quilting Together—Past and Present*. The members of the Young Ladies Sewing Society agreed in 1859 to meet every other week and to "present each member with an album bed quilt with all our names on when they are married. Susie Daggett says she is never going to be married, but we must make her a quilt just the same." Susie often provoked Carrie to laugh so hard she "lost her equilibrium entirely" but in the spring of 1861 laughter faded.

"April 15, 1861. The storm has broken upon us. The Confederates fired on Fort Sumter, just off the coast of South Carolina, and forced her on April 14 to haul down the flag and surrender. President Lincoln has issued a call for 75,000 men and many are volunteering to go all around us. How strange and awful it seems."[18]

Union Baby Quilt, maker unknown, About 1861, Collection of the Museum of American Folk Art, New York; Gift of Phyllis Haders

This quilt with its 34 stars was inspired by two patterns in *Peterson's Magazine* in the summer of 1861. In June the magazine included a sketch for a quilt of stars and stripes and in August an embroidery pattern for the word "Baby." The unknown maker crocheted her little stars and then appliquéd them.

Union Baby Quilt by Barbara Brackman, Lawrence, Kansas, 1996

This update of the 1861 quilt (above) makes good use of the kinds of starred and striped fabrics that are often on the shelves around the 4th of July.

Union Star by Terry Clothier Thompson, Lawrence, Kansas, 1996

Terry Thompson's imaginative quilts combine a variety of symbolic images. A fanciful quilt like this one might have been made for a Union Fair during the War, sold to raise money for the Sanitary Commission or another good cause. Terry has used a floral print for the fields of the flags, a time-saver that gives a different look. The red stripes are appliquéd onto the quilt's background.

Doves represent the hope for peace between North and South as do the entwined Northern Lily and Southern Rose sprouting from the Union shield, an image drawn from Lucy Larcom's *Call to Kansas*. The federal eagle is inspired by the album quilts made in Baltimore in the 1840s and 1850s, which often featured a liberty cap on a pole, a symbol that goes back to the Revolutionary War. Liberty for all is also symbolized in the border of liberty trees. Terry's quilt is a wonderful tour-de-force, a one-of-a-kind piece she hopes will inspire others to exercise their own creativity.

Caroline Richards rode the same waves of patriotic elation followed by the dread that many women North and South knew in the first year of the War. "We have flags on our paper and envelopes, and have all our stationery bordered with red, white, and blue. We wear little flag pins for badges and tie our hair with red, white and blue ribbon and have pins and earrings made of the buttons the soldiers gave us."[19]

Susie Dagget indeed remained single, but as her friends married during the War, members of the Sewing Society pieced blocks in an album pattern and signed the centers with verses reflecting their religion, patriotism, and their hopes for marriage. "Three Rousing Cheers for the Union" reads a block in Mary Fields Fisk's quilt. They also agreed to make a flag quilt for each member whose fiancé served in the Army. The stars on the flag in Abbie Clark's quilt feature inscriptions such as "Enfold them in the Stars and Stripes," and again, "Three Rousing Cheers for the Union."[20]

While Union quilts were in the Northern air, Southern women also expressed their political opinions in patchwork. Annie Darden of Hertford County, North Carolina, working on a quilt in the spring of 1861, wrote in her diary on March 19: "I have finished all the squares for my quilt. I think I shall call it my disunion quilt." Researchers documenting quilts in Arkansas found in the collection of the Arkansas Territorial Restoration a Confederate equivalent to the Union quilt, a red and white striped piece with fields of blue in each corner. In the fields Mrs. Green McPherson of West Point, Arkansas, appliquéd nine stars, two more than the Confederate flag, probably to honor her state, the ninth to secede.[21]

Jemima Ann Thewitts Cook of Fairfield County, South Carolina, designed a "Secession Quilt" that was documented by Myron and Patsy Orlofsky in their 1974 book *Quilts in America*. Cook's granddaughter recalled that Jemima spent six months stuffing and quilting the whitework piece, which features a magnificent center of a column festooned with an eagle and topped by the goddess of liberty. Behind her are the words "Secession" and "1860." The border includes four palmetto trees as shown on South Carolina's state shield.[22]

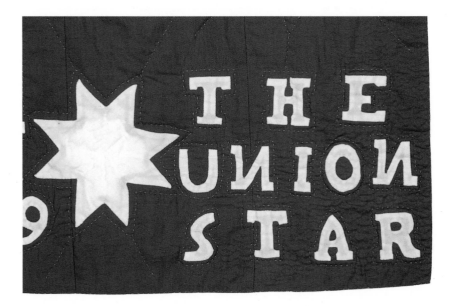

Detail of *Homage to Elizabeth* by Bobbi Finley, San Jose, California, 1996. Full quilt pictured on page 110.

Today we find far more Union quilts than Secession quilts, no surprise since Northern women far outnumbered Southern women. Moreover, it is the victors whose children pass on the stories, so we may have lost the names for many Confederate patterns and their symbolism. After the War Southern men could be arrested for wearing parts of their gray uniform. How many Southern women decided it would be wise to destroy their Secession quilts during Reconstruction in the decades after the War?

Detail of *Union Star* (page 33) by Terry Clothier Thompson, Lawrence, Kansas, 1996

Blue and Gray Battle Quilt

Blue and Gray Battle Quilt by Nancy A. Hornback, Wichita, Kansas, 1996

Nancy Hornback's appliqué quilt was inspired by a Confederate quilt made by Susan Robb in Texas in 1864. It was pictured in *Quilts of the South Texas Plains* from the Prairie Windmill Quilt History and Research Chapter of the National Quilting Association (1986). The center of Robb's quilt featured two troops of Confederate soldiers, each under a different Confederate national flag. Nancy adapted Robb's clever format but placed Union soldiers on one half and Confederates under a Confederate battle flag on the other. The yellow dog follows the officer into battle. In the original a pelican vanquished the eagle, but in Nancy's quilt the Union troops are victorious, so the federal eagle is unchallenged. Robb's quilt was more of a medallion, with floral blocks surrounding the central battle.

Size: 46½" x 46½"
Blocks: 18" finished

FABRIC REQUIREMENTS

- Background and backing: 3⅝ yards. Nancy used a textured print to add interest to the background. Mid-nineteenth-century quilt-makers would have used a good quality plain white cotton (not the unbleached muslin we like for its old look). You can also buy an ecru broadcloth.
- Dogtooth border: ½ yard of solid red cotton. Buy the bluest red you can find, as the old Turkey reds were more of a cherry rather than the tomato red that synthetic dyes produce today.
- Confederate soldier's uniforms: ¼ yard warm gray
- Yankee soldier's uniforms: ¼ yard each of two shades of blue
- Horses: ¼ yard of contrasting browns
- Faces and hands: ¼ yard of a peach, or another brown if you'd like your Union troops to represent the black soldiers.
- Details: Scraps of black for shoes and hair, yellow for the dog, brown for the guns and hair, gray and black for the cannon, gold for gloves and hair, beige and brown for the eagle, and brown for the horses' blankets
- Embellishment: One skein of gold embroidery floss for the stripe on the soldiers' pants (optional). Susan Robb's soldiers wore striped pants. If you can find just the right striped fabrics, you needn't embroider the braid on the uniform pants.
- Confederate battle flag: ⅓ yard each of plain red and ¼ yard of a navy star print. Try to find a star print, or you can appliqué the stars from the template.
- Union flag: ¼ yard each of red and white and ⅛ yard of a little star print for the flag. Nancy used two shades of red for her stripes. Look through the book for alternate ideas for flags.
- Binding: ½ yard (See Binding on page 123.)

CUTTING AND SEWING

Background Blocks

Cut an 18½" x 74 strip from the lengthwise grain of the fabric, then cut it into four 18½" squares. Later you will cut four borders and background from the remaining fabric. The flags are appliquéd onto two of the background blocks and the horses are appliquéd onto the other two.

Flags

The Confederate nation had three official flags between 1861 and 1865; the Union flag was represented in numerous ways. You also might want to picture a particular regiment with their individual battle flag.

Union Flag

Note: This flag is reading right to left because it's flying from a pole on the right. It really isn't backwards (See page 35).

Cut seven 1¼" x 15" strips of red and six 1¼" x 15" strips of white. Alternate strips, starting with red, to make a 10 ¼" x 15" piece.

Appliqué a 4" x 5" rectangle of the navy star print in the right-hand corner of the flag. Cut away the background behind the appliqué to within ¼" of the appliqué stitches. Place the flag in the top left corner of an 18½" block and appliqué the bottom and right edges of the flag to the background. Cut away the background behind the appliqué to within ¼" of the appliqué stitches. The top and left edges become the edges of the 18½" block.

Confederate Battle Flag

Cut a 15" x 10" rectangle of red fabric. Cut two 1⅜" x 20" strips of navy-and-star fabric. Appliqué to the background, lining up the stars. See the photo on page 35. Cut the excess of the navy star strips even with the corners. Place the flag in the top left corner of an 18½" block and appliqué the bottom and right edges of the flag to the background. Cut away the background behind the appliqué to within ¼" of the appliqué stitches. The top and left edges become the edges of the 18½" block.

Enlisted men

Cut the pieces from the appropriate fabrics, adding a ³⁄₁₆" seam allowance for hand appliqué. Appliqué them on top of the flag blocks, noting they overlap the flags. They all face right. Begin by drawing a light pencil line 1½" from the bottom edge of the 18½" block. Start appliquéing with the shoes. Notice that they aren't lined up exactly on the line, but the line is used as a reference point. See the photo on page 35. Continue appliquéing with the pants, shirt, head, hair, cap, rifle, sleeve, and hand. The first man in each parade holds the flag; the others hold their guns.

Officers on Horses

Cut the pieces from the appropriate fabrics, adding a ³⁄₁₆" seam allowance for hand appliqué. Begin by drawing a light pencil line 1½" from the bottom edge of an 18½" block. The Confederate horse faces left; place the hooves on the line and his ear 1" from the left edge of an

1861-1863

The first Confederate flag, the Stars and Bars, with seven stars representing the seceded states, was adopted on March 4, 1861. Two stripes were red, one was white, and the field was blue with white stars.

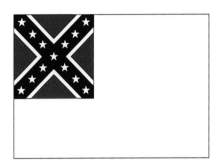

1863-1864

The second Confederate flag, with the square Confederate Battle Flag (the Southern Cross) in the corner, couldn't be mistaken for a Union flag as the Stars and Bars often were. It was hailed as the Stainless Banner because most of it was white. The stars were white, the cross was blue with a white edge, and the triangles were red.

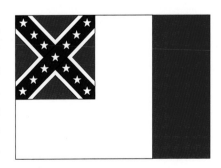

1864-1865

Finally, a red bar was added to the edge of the Stainless Banner because it was too often mistaken for a white flag of surrender.

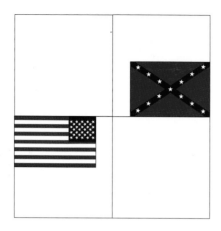

Placement of Flags

Unknown child in a dress with a dogtooth border. Virginia Gunn, who studies both clothing and quilts, has pointed out the similarities in techniques. This appliquéd border is found on many quilts in the mid-nineteenth century.

18½" block. The Union horse faces right; place the hooves on the line and his tail 1" from the left edge of the 18½" block. Appliqué the horses and the officers to the plain 18½" blocks. The blankets are a brown print, with a red strip on the Union blanket and a star on the Confederate blanket. The yellow dog, eagle, and cannon are appliquéd after the border is added.

Setting

Stitch the blocks together with one battle group upside down. See the illustration.

Borders

The four borders are cut from the background fabric and are mitered at the corners. Cut four strips of the background fabric, 5½" x 50". Add to each side, mitering the corners at a 45 degree angle. (See the quilt diagram on page 39.)

Appliqué

After you've added the borders, appliqué the yellow dog behind the Confederate officer and the cannon and eagle as shown on the Union side. These will overlap the seam and border. The gold stripes on the soldiers' uniforms are embroidered in a chain stitch with embroidery floss. Embroider and ink details as you like. See the photo on page 35.

Dogtooth Appliqué Border

You will need four 2" x 50¾" strips. To make these strips, cut six 2" strips the width of the fabric. Cut two 12" long strips from two of the long strips. Stitch one long and one short strip together. Trim to 50¾". Mark the strip with a dot every 1¾" along the edge. Mark and cut a slit 1½" long at each dot. Baste one strip to the edge of the quilt top with the slits facing into the quilt. Appliqué, starting with the second 1¾" unit you marked. Turn under the top edge of each "tooth" ¼", then fold the sides of the tooth to a pyramid, finger pressing as you go. Pin each tooth as you go, or pre-baste. Appliqué each tooth in place. Repeat for the other three sides. The corners will not always come out exactly. That is part of the charm of nineteenth-century quilts. Cut two 4" squares and cut each square in half diagonally. Place the triangle right-side-up over the corner. Refer to the illustration to line up the triangle with the dogtooth border. Appliqué the triangle to the corner. Square up the corner by cutting away the excess triangle fabric. Baste the corners and leave the basting line around the edge of the quilt until you are ready to bind the quilted top.

Quilting

Nancy quilted an outline around each of the figures and filled in the background with a diagonal grid. In the red border she stitched parallel lines following the side of the triangles.

Refer to the General Instructions beginning on page 122 and the photograph for more quilting suggestions and binding.

Mark dots every 1¾."

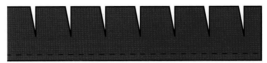

Cut slits 1½" long at each dot.

Fold and appliqué each tooth.

Confederate Flag Star

Union Flag Star

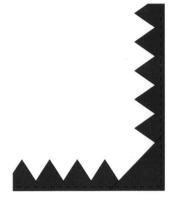

Corner Detail

Cutting Corner Triangles

Note:
The Confederate horse faces left.
The Union horse faces right. Reverse the
pattern before cutting the pieces for the
Union horse.

Horse

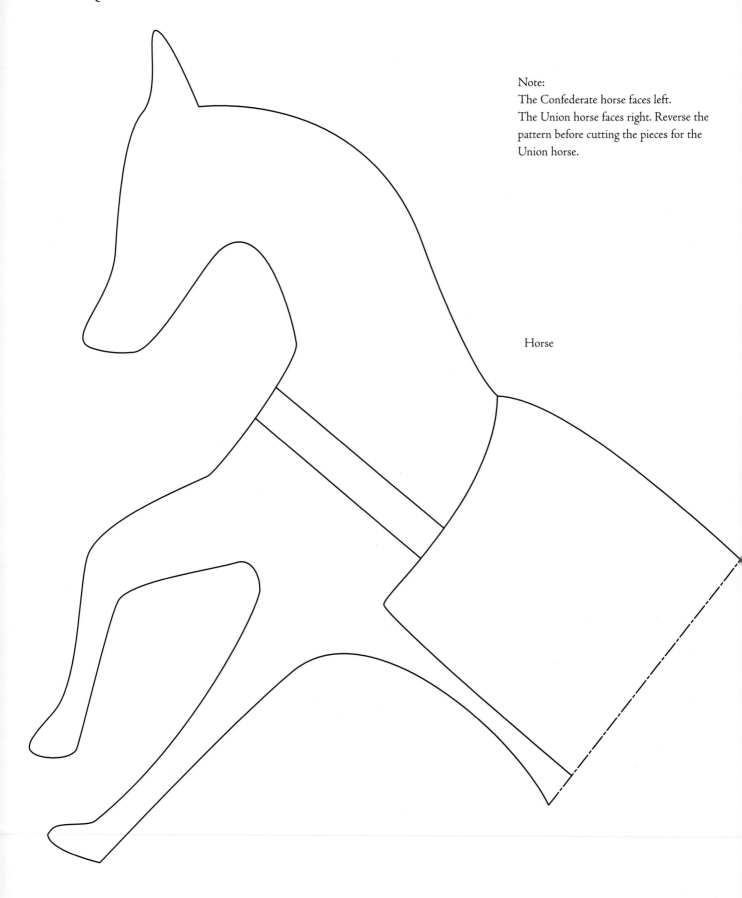

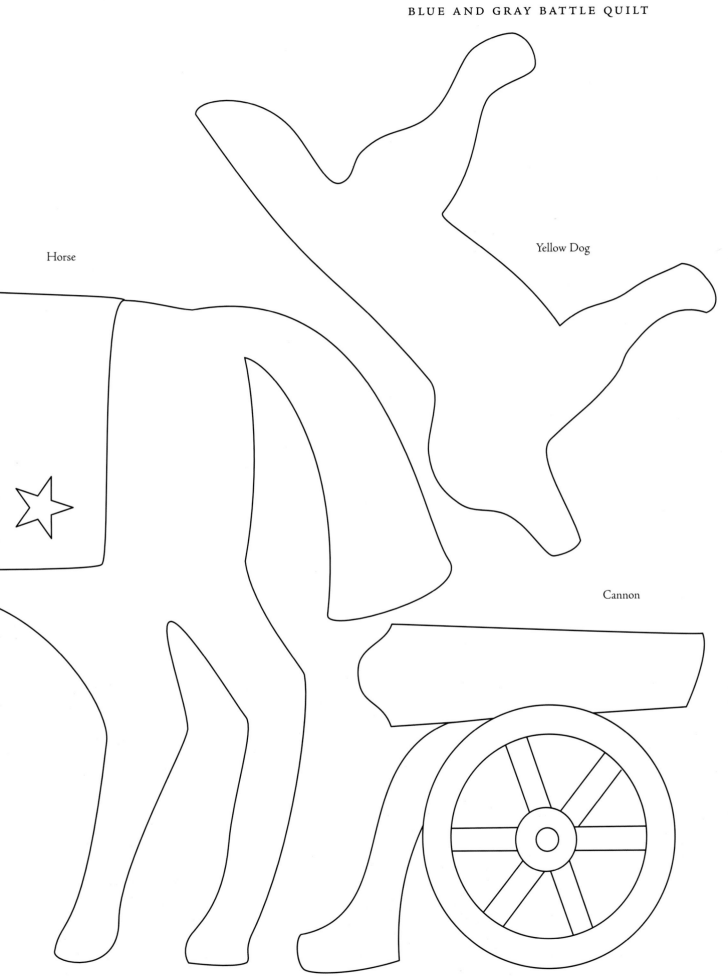

Horse

Yellow Dog

Cannon

Note:
The Confederate officer faces left.
The Union officer faces right. Reverse
the pattern before cutting the pieces
for the Union officer, except the hat
which faces right.

Union Officer Hat

Confederate Officer

Note: All enlisted men face right.

Eagle

Soldier

43

The Constitution and Union Forever

Union quilt by Elizabeth Moffitt Lyle, Kewanee, Illinois, 1860-1864. Collection of the Smoky Hill Museum, Salina, Kansas. Photo courtesy of the Kansas Quilt Project.

Elizabeth Lyle's political sentiments are evident in the Union quilt she made with help from her brother Jack Moffitt, who cut the thirty-three stars. Kansas was the 34th star, admitted on January 29, 1861. Lyle may have made her quilt before that date, working in the fall and into the winter as Lincoln was elected and South Carolina seceded in retaliation. It is obvious she agreed with the Illinois lawyer who campaigned on a promise to uphold the Constitution and the Union. Cherie Ralston has updated Lyle's quilt with a contemporary color scheme and machine piecing techniques.

The Constitution and Union Forever by
Cherie Ralston, Lawrence, Kansas, 1996

Size: 71½″ x 71½″

FABRIC REQUIREMENTS

- Center block background and second and fourth Borders: 4 yards ecru or tan
- Corners: ⅓ yard; Cherie used a darker tan for the corner blocks
- Third border, flowers, buds, and binding: 1⅝ yards red
- Flowers and buds: ¼ yard maroon
- Stars and first border: 2½ yards blue
- Wreath, stems, and leaves: ¾ yard dark green
- A few leaves: scraps medium green
- Flower centers: ⅛ yard goldish brown
- Backing: 4⅛ yards

CUTTING AND SEWING

Center Block

Cut one 36½″ square for the center block. Press the block in half both directions to find the center of the square. Ink or embroider the motto, Constitution and Union Forever, in the center of the square. (See Inking page 125.)

Center Block Appliqué

The center block wreath and stems require six yards of 1½″ bias. To lay out the center wreath, place 2¼ yards of bias to form a circle around the motto with a diameter of 22″ across. Pin the bias in place. Cut four 20″ sections of bias and six 12″ sections of bias for the stems. Following the quilt diagram, lay out the stems, pinning them underneath the bias for the wreath. Appliqué the stems in place. Repeat the procedure for the wreath. Fold under one edge where the bias meets, and finish with small stitches by hand.

Appliqué the roses, buds, stems, and leaves by hand or machine. Cherie's quilt is machine appliquéd. She uses a freezer paper technique.

Trace the templates (without seams) onto the shiny side of the freezer paper (otherwise your patterns will be reversed). Cut them out and iron them shiny side down to the wrong side of the fabric. Cut out adding ³⁄₁₆″ seam allowance. Run a glue stick along the seam allowance and fold the fabric over the paper, leaving no raw edges. Position on the background and pin well. Use thread that matches your appliqué pieces. Adjust your machine to do a blind hem stitch with a very short stitch length and width. Sew right on the edge of the appliqué. Once everything is stitched down, turn the piece over and trim out the underneath fabric within ¼″ of the appliqué stitches. Wet with warm water from a spray bottle and remove the paper. Dry in the dryer or with a dry iron. Always press from the wrong side.

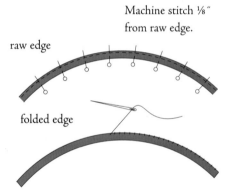

Machine stitch ⅛″ from raw edge.

raw edge

folded edge

Fold over and appliqué.

Terry Thompson uses a fast method to apply the bias for the wreath and stems. Pin bias strips in place on the background. Machine stitch the stems first, ⅛″ from the raw edge of the folded bias. Flip the bias over the raw edges, turn the edge under ⅛″, and appliqué in place by hand or machine, making sure the wreath will cover the stems of the flowers and buds.

Borders

The first border is blue. Cut two 36½″ x 3½″ strips. Add to the top and bottom of the center block. Cut two 42½″ x 3½″ strips lengthwise for the side borders. Add to the sides of the center block.

The second border is ecru. Cut two 42½″ x 3″ lengthwise strips. Add to the top and bottom of the center block. Cut two 47½″ x 3″ lengthwise strips for the side borders. Add to the sides of the center block.

The third border is red. Cut two 47½″ x 3½″ lengthwise strips. Add to the top and bottom of the center block. Cut two 53½″ x 3½″ lengthwise strips for the side borders. Add to the sides of the center block.

The fourth border is two shades of tan. It is pieced, and the stars are appliquéd over the piecing. Measure your quilt top; it should measure 53½″ x 53½″. Cut four 53½″ x 9½″ lengthwise strips (or your measurement) of light tan. Add the top and bottom borders to the quilt top. Then cut four squares of the darker tan that are 9½″ square for the corner posts. Add the darker tan squares to the ends of the side borders and add to the quilt.

Cut 32 blue stars and appliqué to the borders as shown in the quilt diagram. Cherie makes her quilts look lively and spontaneous with tricks like changing the direction of the stars and overlapping stars on the seams of the corner blocks.

Quilting:

Cherie machine quilted a hanging diamond grid in the center (see Utility Quilting page 122), and did meander quilting over the rest of the top. For tips on batting and binding see General Instructions beginning on page 122.

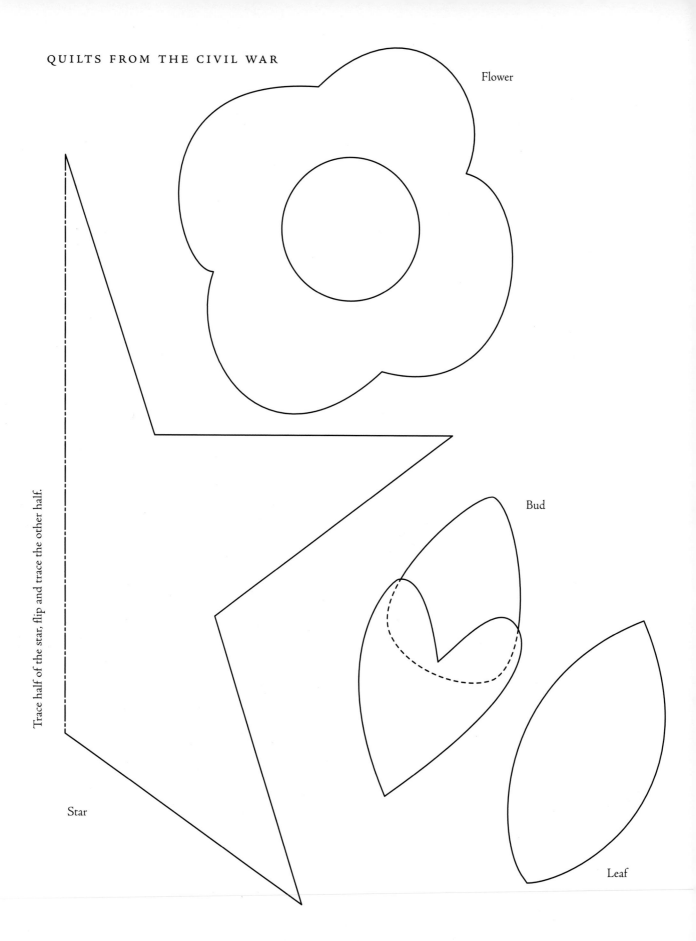

Flower

Bud

Leaf

Trace half of the star, flip and trace the other half.

Star

CHAPTER 4

"Heart and Soul in the Cause," Quilts From Soldiers' Aid Societies

"I have no money nor valuables, my only treasures being my children and I cannot offer them to my country for they are daughters."

Letter to the Mobile *Advertiser and Register*, March 13, 1862[23]

Engraving of people working inside an office of a soldiers' aid society as it appeared in *The Tribute Book* by Frank B. Goodrich, 1865.

Natural dyes do not produce a vivid purple in cotton, but these mid-century blocks show an abundance of prints in the characteristic flat lavender shades available. The autograph album is from Lancaster County, Pennsylvania, as is the *carte-de-visite* (CDV) of the unknown man.

The unknown writer captures the patriotism and frustration of women on both sides. Eager to do something for the cause, they had little to offer but their sons' and husbands' lives, their daughters' dowries, and their own domestic skills. Needlework, chief among their skills, became the war work that most occupied women in the Union and the Confederacy.

Lucy Larcom, abolitionist and feminist, realized that for most women far from battlefields, the war was something experienced "only by the newspapers, by knitting socks for soldiers, and sewing bed-quilts for hospitals." A few independent women might question their rigidly defined roles. Sarah Morgan of Baton Rouge complained often to her diary, "If I was only a man. I don't know a woman here who does not groan over her misfortune in being clothed in petticoats; why can't we fight as well as the men?" Mary Boykin Chesnut wrote of "Kate Heyward, handsome as ever, absolutely jolly, [who] said, 'And can your country find nothing better for you to do than knit stockings for soldiers?'" These independent women were exceptions; most were content to work within their sphere.[24]

When the shooting war began in April, 1861, the armies were ill-prepared. Regiments often required that soldiers supply their own guns, uniforms, and bedding. Many men caught the train to battle with a valued patchwork quilt or a hand-woven blanket in their packs, a theme expressed in the song *Take Your Gun and Go, John.*

Soldier's Sixteen Patch by Linda Frost, Lawrence, Kansas, 1996.

> "*The army's short of blankets, John,*
> *Then take this heavy pair.*
> *I spun and wove them when a girl*
> *And work'd them with great care,*
> *A rose in ever corner, John,*
> *And here's my name, you see!*
> *On the cold ground they'll warmer feel*
> *Because they're made by me.*"[25]

Elizabeth Skiles Ward's wedding quilt

Rally Round the Flag, Boys by Wava A. Stoker-Musgrave and Terry Clothier Thompson, Lenexa and Lawrence, Kansas, 1996

Major Lemuel Ward of Garysburg, North Carolina, took his wife's wedding quilt with him. Like many other Confederate officers he marched off to war in the style to which he was accustomed, accompanied by a slave who prepared his meals and served them with the family's sterling silver flatware. Elizabeth Skiles Ward's tulip appliqué was spread on the ground each night and, remarkably, the quilt survived the war with the Major.[26]

Women sent their handmade bedding with the men they loved, but soon realized that the rebellion might last longer than the ninety days for which their soldiers had enlisted. They quickly mobilized to form Soldiers' Aid Societies. The majority were organized in the North, where women had a history of plying their needles for causes from abolition and anti-prostitution campaigns to clothing the town's poor.

Caroline Cowles Richards documented the immediacy of women's response in her diary.

"May, 1861. Many of the young men are going from Canandaigua and all the neighboring towns. It seems very patriotic and grand when they are singing, 'It is sweet, Oh, 'tis sweet, for one's country to die,' and we hear the martial music and see the flags flying and see the recruiting tents on the square and meet men in uniform at every turn and see train loads of the boys in blue going to the front, but it will not seem so grand if we hear they are dead on the battlefield, far from home. . . . We are going to sew for them in our society. . . . We are going to write notes and enclose them in the garments to cheer up the soldier boys."[27]

51

Detail of *Rally Round the Flag, Boys* by Wava A. Stoker-Musgrave and Terry Clothier Thompson, Lenexa and Lawrence, Kansas, 1996

Linda Frost printed fabric with a fanciful Sanitary Commission logo for her classmates, so Terry and Wava included a label on their interpretation of a soldier's quilt. Full quilt pictured on page 51.

Women all over the north converted their sewing and social societies to war work and organized new ones. Emily Hawley Gillespie of Iowa wrote in her diary on December 3, 1861. "A number of ladies met to form a society; we named it the Soldier's Relief Society." In St. Louis, Sarah Jane Full Hill recalled: "Every loyal household became a soldier's aid society. . . . We immediately set to work and made the sewing machine hum night and day. Mother, my aunt and we four older girls worked unceasingly and soon had a large box filled and ready to send to our soldier boys. We made bed ticks which could be filled with hay or straw, could be easily emptied and refilled and took up but little room on a march. We made and tied comforters thick and warm. . . . And we made quantities of flannel shirts and kept the knitting needles clicking, fashioning socks and mittens. How the boys rejoiced over the contents of that box, the forerunner of several during the winter."[28]

Some women, like the Full family, supplied their own soldier and his company. Others made clothing and bedding for unknown men. Efforts of many Northern women were coordinated by the United States Sanitary Commission. This group of men, modeled after an English organization that had pioneered sanitary hospitalization during the Crimean War, initially formed to act as an advocate for better field and hospital conditions for the soldiers. The United States Sanitary Commission added the distribution of supplies to their list of goals when women overwhelmed their offices with clothing, bedding, and medical materials. Women quickly moved into positions of authority in the auxiliary of the Commission as they organized branch offices all over the north to process the donations, which arrived in amazing quantities.

The women's activities of the Sanitary Commission began in New York City at a meeting at the Cooper Union (also called the Cooper Institute.) Charlotte Wilson, visiting from New Hampshire, wrote to her father: New York May 15, 1861. "I went this morning to the Cooper Institute to see the operation of an admirably organized society for the relief and aid of the sick and wounded soldiers. . . . Several of my particular friends are members of this Society. They have to work very hard, answering notes from people in the country, receiving contributions, etc. This morning while I was there a poor man, belonging to the Middle Classes, came in with two enormous bundles. He said 'he was a poor man, but his wife and he wanted to do something,' so he brought a donation of four dozen sheets, all new and nicely made, three dozen pillow cases. 57 pincushions. Besides lint etc. wasn't that generous? It gives you some idea of the enthusiasm which pervades all classes."[29]

While at the school, Charlotte might have made the acquaintance of Abby Woolsey, who wrote her sister two days later, "I am going to the Cooper Union today to try and get some simple pattern for calico gowns. They advertise to supply paper patterns of garments to ladies."[30]

United States Sanitary Commission Logo

The Sanitary Commission supplied more than patterns for soldier's clothing. Six months after the war began the group furnished "some plain directions" to the "woman whose heart is stirred with yearning to do something in her own town." She should "go to two or three of her neighbors and take counsel. . . . Then let the ladies form themselves into a Soldiers' Relief Circle, to meet once a week from 1 to 4 P.M.—the time to be spent in sewing or knitting for the soldier . . . each lady simply pledging herself to give three hours per week, either in the meeting, or at home, to the service of the soldier." The Commission recommended that each group "form a Committee on Supplies—to solicit donations, in kind from stores, farmers, and citizens in general, in yarn, wool, cotton cloth, and other articles, to be made up by the industry of the Circle." The local groups were to ship a monthly package and a monthly report to the agency. [31]

The activities of the Sanitary Commission are well-documented in its own histories and in the words of women of the day. Most local organizations in the Union operated under their umbrella, but a second group, the Christian Commission, developed parallel services with hospital oversight and donations of food, clothing, bedding, and medical aid. Unlike the Sanitary Commission, which favored secular aid, the Christian Commission offered religious and moral counseling. During the War the Sanitary and Christian Commissions were rivals for money and women's time. After the War the majority of published biographies

A sketch of the Women's Meeting at the Cooper Union Hall to organize the Women's Central Association of Relief, the first women's auxiliary of the Sanitary Commission. From *Frank Leslie's Illustrated.*

Detail *Sanitary Comission Nine-Patch*
made by Sharon Durken Rush, Glencoe,
Minnesota, 1996

Sherry's faithful copy of a Sanitary
Commission quilt includes an inked label
to represent the stamp the U.S.S.C. used.
All Sanitary Commission donations were
stamped to prevent theft. For a photograph
and instructions for this quilt see project
instructions beginning on page 61.

and histories favored the Sanitary Commission, so it is this organization and its quilts that are best remembered.

In her study of quilts for Union soldiers, Virginia Gunn estimates
125,000 quilts and comforts were distributed by the Sanitary
Commission during the war. Certainly quilts were among their top
requests. An 1861 request for donations listed "Quilts, of cheap material,
about seven feet long by fifty inches wide." Another directive wanted
"comfortables 8 feet long, 4 feet wide, of cheap, dark prints, wadded with
cotton." Surviving soldier's quilts are extremely rare, but from them and
the recorded descriptions we can guess that most were narrow, useful for
a cot, a bedroll, or a hospital bed. They were probably simple patchwork
designs, pieced of the calicoes that were relatively inexpensive at the
time. Checks and brown prints, cheap and dark enough to hide dirt,
would have been popular. Shirting prints (small figures on white) and
a variety of dress scraps would also be included. The quilts may have
been tied or quilted rather minimally. Northern women did much other
needlework for the soldiers, especially knitting socks and sewing clothing, but piecing quilts and comforters seems to have been a primary
activity on the home front. [32]

Checks and plaids were popular in clothing as worn by these twins in a *carte-de-
visite* photograph. Are they girls wearing
fashionable Zouave jackets or could they
be little boys just waiting for the day their
curls are cut and they no longer have to
wear skirts over their pants?

> ★ ★ ★ ★
>
> # DESCRIPTION OF ARTICLES MOST WANTED
>
> Blankets for single beds • Quilts of cheap materials, about seven feet
> long by fifty inches wide • Knit woolen socks • Woolen or Canton
> flannel bedgowns, wrappers, undershirts, & drawers • Slippers
>
> . . . All articles should be closely packed in wooden boxes, or in very strongly wrapped
> bales, and clearly directed. On the top of the contents of each box, under the cover,
> a list of what it contains should be placed; a duplicate of this list should be sent by
> mail, addressed to the U.S. Sanitary Commission.
>
> ★ ★ ★ ★

Why have so few survived? They were not masterpieces, and we can
imagine that few actually made it home.

Because the victorious Union wrote much of the history of the Civil
War, we know far less about the work of Confederate women. Yet so many
Southern diarists, most of whom were of the planter class (the agricultur-
al aristocracy), mention war work that we can draw some conclusions.

Many Southern women met to sew with extended family, slaves, and close friends, unlike Northern women, who met regularly in public sewing rooms to cooperate with community members who might have been strangers to them before the War. Southern women had little experience with public groups such as "sewing circles and other useful Yankee inventions," as popular novelist Mrs. E.D.E.N. Southworth had phrased it before the War. Many of the Southern gentry felt that such groups were unladylike. Mary Chesnut reported two conversations with gentlemen who disapproved of women of their class working for the Confederacy. "Captain Shannon . . . seemed to find my knitting a pair of socks a day for the soldiers droll in some way. The yarn is coarse. He has been so short a time away from home he does not know how the poor soldier needs them." Frank Hampton was more specific in his concerns. "Are you in for the frenzied patriotic style? . . . I mean do you knit socks and join associations with lots of vulgar people? The ladies of Charleston have voted that sort of thing down. They leave it to the lower orders' . . . "Chesnut's opinion of Hampton's snobbery is revealed in a later characterization; she called him "the driveler at the dinner table." Her friend Mary Preston put him in his place that night. "You are under a delusion in some way—but if it is vulgar to love one's country and to be willing to do all one can for it, I am a vulgar patriot."[33]

Hampton may have spoken for Charleston's old families, but nearly every woman's words record some handwork for the soldiers. Women at every level made clothing. Late in the war Chesnut and a friend "paid our respect to Mrs. [Robert E.] Lee. Her room was like an industrial school—everybody so busy. Her daughters were all there, plying their needles, and some other ladies. . . . And when we came out, "Did you see how the Lees spend their time? What a rebuke to the taffy parties!" First Lady Varina Davis, distraught over the Southern losses, wrote Chesnut in October, 1864, of her anguish. "I cannot read—but I sew hard."[34]

Many Southern white women were at a disadvantage in the first months of the war because they had no practical sewing experience. Lucy Breckenridge, a Virginia girl, wrote in her diary: "November 26, 1862. On Monday we all went hard to work making shirts for the soldiers and I made the first whole garment that I have made in many years—since I used to play babies." Lucy and her sisters of the planter class relied on their servants to do menial work. Plain sewing, the construction of clothing and household linens, was the type of work relegated to slaves in a well-organized household. The lack of sewing skills is a consistent theme during and after the war when the slaves had gone and their "missus" could not afford to hire the skilled seamstresses to come back to work for wages. In general, Southern women did not value plain sewing as the Northern women did, and their efforts to aid their soldiers were hampered at first by their lack of skills.[35]

A fashionable young woman dressed much like 16-year-old Caroline Cowles Richards must have been when she wrote in her diary in February, 1859. "It is nice, though to dress in style and look like other people. I have a Garibaldi waist and a Zouave jacket and a Balmoral skirt." The Garibaldi waist (what we would call a shirt) had full sleeves that showed to good effect under the Zouave jacket, cut open in the front. Garibaldi was an Italian revolutionary who united his country in 1861. The Zouaves were exotically dressed French soldiers in the Crimean War of the mid-1850s. The Balmoral skirt was a plaid, inspired by Queen Victoria's Balmoral Castle in Scotland, began in 1853.

The most significant difference between the two cultures was the lack of sewing materials in the Confederacy. The reason so few Southern quilts made during the war have survived is that far fewer were made. Women were short of fiber to weave fabric, and even thread to sew. Cotton was the major Southern crop, but the well-established system dictated that raw fiber went north to New England mills or across the ocean to European countries for processing into cloth and sewing thread. William Tecumseh Sherman taunted a Southern friend in late 1860, "The North can make a steam engine, locomotive or railway car; hardly a yard of cloth or a pair of shoes can you make." [36]

This woman is dressed in the everyday fabrics from which many utilitarian quilts were made.

Women in the Confederacy also formed Soldier's Aid Societies, but without the formal organization of a central Sanitary or Christian Commission. Catherine Devereux Edmonston, who lived on Looking Glass Creek northeast of Raleigh, North Carolina, made many diary entries about her aid work in the first two years of the war. On April 29, 1861, two weeks after Fort Sumter, she reported she was working with neighborhood women to make fatigue uniforms for the troops. Into early May she organized a group of seven women slaves who sewed uniforms and tents on her piazza (the multi-storied side porch of the Southern house). Through the open window she "could hear their comments on the 'War' & the 'Cloth House' they were making for their Master to sleep under." In July, after a trip to Charleston, she noted that "The Ladies all over the country had formed themselves in Hospital associations & were at work on quilted comfortables, shirts, drawers, etc for the sick & wounded. The hearts of the whole population were fired—& could Lincoln & Seward have seen with what unanimity & self abnegation they acted they must have been shaken at least in their ideas of conquest." [37]

Mary Boykin Chesnut joined an aid association in Richmond, Virginia, during the summer of 1861. Frank as always, she recorded the dissension among the doyennes of Confederate society.

"August 18, 1861. The ladies were old ones and all wanted their own way. . . . One of the causes of disturbance: Mrs. Randolph proposed to divide everything sent us equally with the Yankee wounded and sick prisoners. Some were enthusiastic from a Christian point of view. Some shrieked in wrath."

"September 2, 1861: Small war in the Ladies Aid Society. . . already secession is in the air. . . . At first there were nearly a hundred members . . . now ten or twenty are all they can show. The worst is, they have forgotten the hospitals, where they really could do so much good, and gone off to provision and clothe the army. A drop in the bucket—or ocean." [38]

The minutes of the Greenville Ladies Association in Aid of the Volunteers of the Confederate Army, published sixty years ago, lack Chesnut's candidness, but they tell us much about the activities of a southern soldier's aid association. Formed in July, 1861, the South

Carolina group sent a box to soldiers within a week. The women refurbished an old school building on College Street into a Soldier's Rest, a hospice for injured and ill men traveling through the city. There they met weekly to cut out clothing, bedding, and comforters, which volunteers took home to sew. In the first year of the War quilts were an important part of their work. On Christmas Eve in 1861 the Association bought 118 yards of calico from which they cut 12 comforts to send home with seamstresses. Between July, 1861, and July, 1862, they recorded 64 comforts and comforters in the stock of bedding, supplies, and clothing kept on hand to benefit soldiers in their own hospital and others.[39]

The woven stripes, checks and plaids in these antique blocks and top were very common in the everyday quilts of the Civil War era. They were inexpensive and colorfast. The green check and the brown were quite popular. People called them apron checks.

Union military strategists had immediately sent ships to blockade Southern ports, breaking the Southern circle of exported raw material and imported finished goods. As months of blockade dragged into years, Confederate women were hard pressed to do any sewing at all.

Sarah Watkins of Carroll County, Mississippi, recorded the activities of the Middleton Soldiers' Aid Society, which formed in July, 1861. She and her daughter attended every Wednesday, but there was little work to do, owing to the shortage of cloth and yarn. By February the sewing society had adjourned and Sarah complained that "Goods are very scarce and dear." Judith McGuire's parlor group eventually abandoned their sewing machines and returned to hand-sewing when they ran out of manufactured thread, because their machines tangled the cotton thread they could spin themselves.[40]

Catherine Edmonston continued to sew for the soldiers despite the shortages. In late 1862 she cut up every expendable piece of cloth in the house and slave quarters to outfit six soldiers. "I can by using my table covers, scraps of flannel, etc., manage to piece out six flannel shirts. . . . I can I think spare two blankets more and will take my chintz coverlids and make four comfortables." She finished two more shirts by making a

57

"small piece of flannel do duty for a large one & by piecing & putting collars and cuffs of different colours," and eventually "Suceeded yesterdy in getting my tenth woolen shirt for our soldiers, tho the cover of my sofa pillow went to make out the sleeves!"[41]

Unable to obtain manufactured cotton yardgoods, some Southerners relied on homewoven fabrics, usually a fabric of locally-grown wool combined with cotton or linen. Once the clothing only of slaves and rural whites, homewoven grays, plaids, and checks eventually became the fabric of the planter class as well as the uniforms of Southern soldiers. (See Chapter 6 for more about home fabric production.) When Southerners returned to time-consuming tasks of spinning and weaving fabric by hand, quilts became a luxury. There are precious few Southern references to quilts made for soldiers, like Catherine Edmonston's mention of her chintz quilts recycled into comforters. The literature I examined shows no surviving quilts made specifically as Confederate soldier's aid projects, but some must have survived somewhere in the South as souvenirs of the Lost Cause.

Three years into the war, activities dwindled. "December 5, 1864. As the funds of the Society are becoming exhausted, it was proposed and adopted that a Xmas supper should be given for its benefit." But it wasn't only funds that were exhausted; the women of Greenville had come to realize that defeat was on the horizon. They no longer had enthusiasm or fabric for the cause. In January members voted to contact "Dr. Boyce and request him to deliver an address for the purpose of re-exciting the interest of the community in this Society, and of encouraging the attendance upon its meetings, all our efforts having failed." The spring brought waves of Union troops to overrun South Carolina. The last entry in the minutes is for May 1st. "No meeting on account of the Yankee Raiders, who stripped the 'Rest' of every article it contained, leaving the Society without the means of carrying on any farther (sic) operations."[42]

Official histories of the Northern Soldiers' Aid Associations occasionally allude to an unintended role as a lonelyhearts club: "Sometimes there would be found in the toes of a sock a letter addressed, 'To the soldier who shall wear these socks:'Be of good cheer! May these socks keep your feet warm, while you stand on your post, or march on to battle and victory!' 'May the rebellion soon be subdued, and you have the satisfaction of having aided in the glorious work.' Sometimes quite lengthy epistles would be folded up in these presents, with the names and address of the writers given, and we have known some very pleasant correspondence to follow from these friendly missives to the soldiers."[43]

The boxes North and South must have inspired numerous romances, a few of which are documented. Cornelia Colton was an eighteen-year-old clerk who worked for the government in Columbus, Ohio. She described the beginnings of her correspondence with a soldier in Kansas inspired by a note in the toe of a sock. "Dear Mother. I received a long letter from Father yesterday morning enclosing one from Fort Leavenworth. No one could have been more surprised than I was, for I had actually forgotten all about that pair of socks. 'Twas a good letter wasn't it? and I think deserves an answer. . . . Sheldon thinks it is 'one of the romantic incidents of the war' and says he can find out something about the young or old man who wrote that. I think he showed good judgment . . . [and] did not seem to be of the class of young men who wish to 'exchange photographs.' "

A few letters traveled between Kansas and Ohio, but by spring mention of the soldier disappears from the family correspondence. It may be that too many Coltons were involved in approving Nelia's correspondence. "I have received another letter from our Soldier at Ft. Leavenworth. I will bring it home with me, and also the reply that I intend to make. It is very embarrassing to think that a third person is to read the letters one writes." [44]

Fannie Chester, a sixteen-year-old living in Vernon, Connecticut, helped make quilts for the Sanitary Commission to distribute in 1864. She enclosed a note with one listing members of the Vernon Patriotic Society who had worked on it. She added her address as she signed her name and that of her little sister, Lissie C. Their quilt made its way to the branch office of the Sanitary Commission to be inventoried and sent to a central distribution office. Fannie's quilt finally arrived in the hands of twenty-seven-year-old Captain Robert Emmett Fisk, with the 132nd New York Volunteer Infantry in North Carolina. Glad for a blanket and an opportunity to write to a young woman, Fisk sent letters to both Fannie and Lissie C. from New Berne. "Miss Fannie Chester: This is to show that I am the recipient, through the U.S. Sanitary Commission of the Patchwork bed cover or quilt, which you had a hand in constructing. I am deeply sensible of the obligation I am under to you and your fair companions for this your contribution to my comfort." Fisk closed with an invitation to write again, "I should be much please (sic) to hear that this note reached you in safety."

Fannie, realizing she had overstepped the boundaries of propriety by being so bold as to solicit mail from a stranger, asked her older sister Elizabeth to explain the situation.

"Vernon, Oct. 3rd, 1864

Capt. R.E. Fisk,

A few days since, I had the pleasure of receiving two letters written by you addressed to my sisters, Miss Fannie Chester, and Lissie C. Corbin. The former being at present busily engaged in school duties and the latter having reached the very mature age of (to use her own words) 'two old last July,' I have been deputed to answer the said communications. . . ."

Fisk asked Elizabeth to continue the correspondence herself. Despite anxiety that her letters might be "made subject of ridicule" in the camp, she decided to write, justifying her boldness by explaining that "we at home are urged to write to our friends in the army, to cheer them in their loneliness, and to atone, in some measure, for the hardships they undergo for us." Romance blossomed over sister Fanny's quilt. After the truce Robert visited Elizabeth, and they married to live, as we can guess from Elizabeth's letters, rather happily ever after.[45]

Soldier's Four Patch by Linda Frost, Lawrence, Kansas, 1996.

Sanitary Commission Nine-Patch

Sanitary Commission Nine-Patch by Sharon
Durken Rush, Glencoe, Minnesota, 1996

Thousands of quilts similar to this must have been made during the War, but only two seem to have survived. Sherri Rush copied an original Sanitary Commission Nine-Patch quilt as closely as she could, using reproduction prints to imitate each of the forty blocks.[46]

Size: 44½″ x 66½″
Blocks: 6″ finished

FABRIC REQUIREMENTS

- Nine-Patch blocks: The 40 blocks will require a large variety of fat quarters or a total of 1½ yards in reproduction cottons to achieve a scrap look in the quilt. You'll want a contrast of light and dark fabrics.
- Nine-Patch center: ¼ yard off-white
- Setting strips and borders. Three different browns were used to get the thrown-together look that is so typical of utilitarian quilts in this era. You will need 2 yards for the setting strips between the nine-patches, 2 yards for the side borders and 1⅜ yards for the top and bottom borders.
- Backing: Use the fabrics leftover from the setting strips and side borders for the backing. Pieced together backs are typical of the era.
- Binding: ½ yard (See Binding page 123.)

CUTTING AND SEWING

Nine-Patch Blocks

For the 40 nine-patch blocks you will need 160 light 2½″ squares, 160 dark 2½″ squares, and 40 off-white 2½″ squares. Use the cutting method that is easiest for you, either a 2½″ template or strip cutting. Make 40 nine-patch blocks.

Inking

They stamped their indentification on every donation. The official logo of the USSC and the type of lettering that might be on a quilt from Wisconsin. SAS means the Soldier's Aid Society. (See Inking page 123-124). Ink one off-white 2½″ square with the logo of the Sanitary Commission.

Setting Strips

The nine-patch blocks are set together with thirty-five horizontal strips cut 2½″ x 6½″. Before you cut, notice that Sherri has cut both the horizontal and vertical setting strips so the stripe in the fabric runs from top to bottom. Stitch five rows using eight nine-patches and seven horizontal setting strips. See the quilt diagram.

Measure all of your sewn rows; they should measure 62½″ and cut four vertical setting strips 62½″ by 2½″. Adjust the length of the strips if your measurements are different, but choose one measurement to cut and ease the other rows to fit. Stitch together following the quilt diagram.

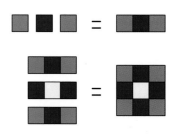

Piecing of Nine-Patch Block

Side borders

Measure the length of your top vertically through the middle. It should measure 62½". Cut two 62½" (or your measurement) x 3½" strips. Add to the sides.

Top and Bottom Borders

Measure the width of your top horizontally through the middle. It should measure 44½". Cut two 44½" (or your measurement) x 2½" strips. Add the top and bottom borders. Sherri copied the original as closely as she could, which meant she didn't worry about lining up her blocks and setting strips. If you prefer a more precision set, measure and stitch carefully.

For tips on batting, utility quilting, and binding see the General Instructions beginning page 122.

Tips for Reproduction Fabrics

The dark, cheap cottons the Sanitary Commission asked for were probably brown prints in the madder dyes of the era. Madder, a vegetable dye, produces a wide range of warm shades that range from a rusty red through burnt orange to a purplish chocolate brown color (called puce), and a brown so dark it's almost black. New England mills sold such browns fairly cheaply, and these were the cottons that were the material of women's everyday clothing; the dresses they did not wear on the street or to receive callers. Look for the warm brown calicoes available today. Avoid greenish-browns; they look more like the end-of-the-century browns.

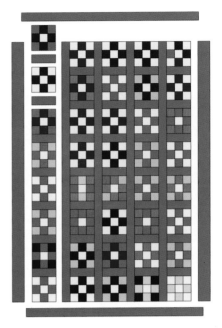

Quilt Top Construction

CHAPTER 5

"The Hearts and Hands of the People,"
Fairs on the Home Front

"For the benefit of the sick and wounded soldiers, a fair will open on Monday,
Feb 22, 1864 . . . under the favorable direction of the patriot daughters, assisted
by a number of gentlemen of the city and county of Lancaster, for the exhibition
and sale of goods, wares, manufactures and products of every description—
agricultural, mechanical, artistical, fanciful and useful. Ladies' Handiwork in
great variety, Books, Maps, Prints, Pictures and Notions of all sorts, being the
accumulated stock of donations and contributions made and forthcoming from
the Hearts and Hands of the People."

From a broadside in the collection of Lancaster County Historical Society,
Lancaster, Pennsylvania

Women in uniform and their beaux at a photo booth at the Sanitary Fair held in Chicago in 1863. The booth may have sold photographs of generals and famous people, or a photographer may have volunteered to make *carte-de-visite* portraits of fair-goers for the cause. Courtesy of the Chicago Public Library.

Flag by Wava A. Stoker-Musgrave,
Lenexa, Kansas, 1996

Serpentine stripes like those in this
reproduction print were fashionable for
clothing, furnishings, and quilts in the
mid-nineteenth century. The image of the
U.S. flag, so standardized today, was more
flexible in the past. Drawings and needlework often picture unique variations.
Handmade flags, especially silk flags,
were good sellers at fairs during the War.

An Englishman described the first Christmas in the Confederacy at a plantation near Charleston. The daughters of the house, citizens of newly seceded South Carolina, told their father they preferred cash to the jewelry and gifts he usually bought them. The planter reported proudly, "They wanted to give it to the State to help arm and equip some of the military companies. I couldn't let them suffer for their patriotism, you know; so I had to advance the money and buy trinkets too." [47]

Women could wheedle money from the men who held the purse strings and donate their trinkets to the cause, but as always, many looked to their needlework for a source of money. We have seen how abolitionists raised money with their Freedom's Fairs in Chapter 1. Before the War much Fair money also went to Protestant church causes, as it does today. Millie Gray lived in Virginia and wrote of Fairs in her diary. In November, 1833: "The Agricultural Show took place today—and the Presbyterian ladies had a fair. . . . I went up at night to the Fair with the children." [48]

Sarah Josepha Hale, the editor of the important magazine *Godey's Lady's Book*, and a nineteenth-century trend setter, advocated Ladies' Fairs as acceptable events that fell within women's sphere. But some objected to women stooping to commercialism of any kind.

Rebecca Gratz, a wealthy Philadelphian, wrote her sister-in-law in 1834, "Mothers & prudes were shocked that young & Innocent girls should be bartering pin cushions & smiles at these sanctified tables at an expense of modesty far beyond the price of gold." William Tecumseh Sherman might not be classified often with the prudes, but in a letter to his wife Ellen he let her know his feelings about Fairs. "I don't approve of ladies selling things at table. So far as superintending the management of such things, I don't object, but it merely looks unbecoming for a lady to stand behind a table to sell things. Still, do as you please." [49]

The descriptions of mid-nineteenth-century Fairs generally include

65

Cut-out-Chintz Crib Quilt by Shirley and Shirlene Wedd, Lawrence, Kansas, 1996-7

From about 1760 to 1860 American quilters loved to cut up a piece of floral chintz and rearrange the flowers, birds, and baskets on a quilt top. We often call these *Broderie Perse* quilts (French for Persian Embroidery), but we find no record of that term during the Civil War years. The Wedds, mother and daughter, have interpreted a crib quilt made by Martha Jane Singleton Hatter Bullock (1815-1896) of Greensboro, Alabama, who donated similar chintz quilts to the Gunboat Fairs in Tuscaloosa and Marion. For more information on Martha's quilts see *Alabama Gunboat Quilts*, by Bryding Adams.

references to women indulging in commercial enterprise. Ada Bacot in Society Hill, South Carolina, summarized such an event in her diary entry for Sept 17, 1861, "Our fair is over and we have been much more successful than we expected, every thing was disposed of and most of the articles sold very well. I helped Hannah Waring & Mrs. Porcher with their table at which we made $75. I met a good many of my friends and had a very nice day." [50]

Once the fighting began, Confederate women realized their new country needed every widow's mite to buy arms and equipment. Late in the first year of the War they dedicated their fundraising efforts to a specific cause, purchasing gunboats for the Confederate Navy. Alarmed and antagonized by the Union capture of Port Royal, South Carolina, in November, 1861, women in New Orleans held the first of the Gunboat Fairs. As Naval battles raged on the coasts and rivers, the idea flashed across the Confederacy with Gunboat Fairs, festivals, and patriotic events during the spring of 1862. Mary Boykin Chesnut recorded one event in Richmond, Virginia, for which she gave "the girls a string of pearls to be raffled for the gunboat fair.... Our fair is in full blast. We keep a restaurant.... We have made bushels of money. All the world came." [51]

Unknown girl in a delaine dress.

Her dress looks to be *mousseline de laine*, a fabric popular for clothing and quilts in the 1850s and 1860s. The fabric was a combination weave of wool and cotton. The French words mean a wool muslin, a term most Americans shortened to "delaine." The fine woven fabric enabled mills to print nicely detailed designs. This dress features the small florals so popular at the time. Each figure is isolated and repeated in a half-drop fashion, which means they form a diagonal grid. Costume historian Virginia Gunn has pointed out how the diagonal grid was in vogue for both quilts and fabric.

Jewelry was not the only big-ticket item donated. E. Bryding Adams has studied the role of quilts at these Southern Fairs. She has found records of six quilts donated to Alabama fairs to be raffled, and also records a Mobile woman's offer to donate her sewing machine to the gunboat fund. [52]

The gunboats at the heart of the cause cost about $80,000 each. Inspired by the success of the css *Virginia*, a confiscated iron-clad formerly named for Merrimack, New Hampshire, Southern strategists realized that new technology might make up for small numbers and became determined to build iron-clad rams. Enthusiasm for the ladies' gunboats was quickly tempered by Confederate losses of ports in Virginia and finally of New Orleans in April. The captain of the css *Virginia* sank the ship in May to avoid Union capture. These disappointing events probably inspired Mary Chesnut to wail to her diary in early June: "Oh that we had given our thousand dollars to the hospital and not to the gunboat." [53]

Interest in Gunboat Fairs waned after 1862, but during that year the women of the Confederacy through their Fairs and donations raised enough money to buy three ships—the *Georgia*, the *Fredericksburg*, and the *Charleston*. The *Georgia*, commissioned in 1863, protected the port of Savannah and captured nine Union ships. The *Fredericksburg* patrolled Richmond's James River throughout the War. In a losing contest, the ladies' gunships played the game of thwarting Union raids and keeping the enemy busy for years.

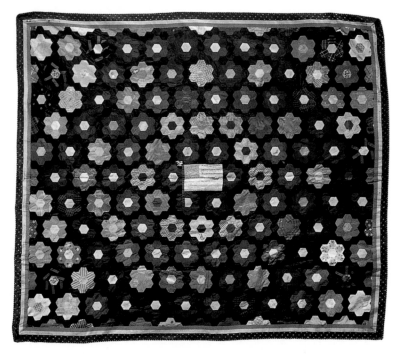

Union women relied on the government to provide the arms and equipment for battle. They directed their fundraising energies to supplying items for the comfort of the soldier and the care of the wounded and ill.

May, the youngest of the Woolsey family, was one of many little girls who imitated their elders. Her Aunt Abby wrote May's mother in March of 1862 that she "is busy concocting things for a fair she and Bertha hold to-day, for the benefit of our "BRAVE VOLUNTEERS" Papa and mamma and aunties are to buy the things, and May is to spend the money on little books (for the hospital library)." [54]

Fairs became a way of life for many on the home front. Sewing, glueing, and knitting for fairs occupied women waiting for news of loved ones, and fairs gave new excitement to causes that had long ceased to

Silk Autograph Quilt by Mary Hughes Lord, Nashville, Tennessee, about 1860, 72″ x 83″, Collection of the Smithsonian Institution, Photo # 74-896

When Tennessee seceded in June, 1861, Union loyalists like the family of 13-year-old Mary Hughes fled north. Before the war she had begun the silk hexagon quilt, in a pattern that was a typical learning project for a girl. On the day of secession she appliquéd the flag in the center.

In mid-1862 the Hughes returned to Nashville, re-occupied by Union troops. There Mary met General William S. Rosecrans who suggested she collect autographs on the quilt. His was the first. Over the next twenty years or so Mary diligently asked famous people from Abraham Lincoln to Theodore Roosevelt for their signatures. The quilt appeared at Lincoln's and President Garfield's funerals and was "hung out at different Inaugurations," according to the note Mary left with it. In 1943, her daughter donated the quilt to the Smithsonian. This is exactly the kind of quilt sold at many a Civil War Fair. Re-enactors might want to follow Mary Huges Lord's lead and bring an autograph quilt with them to re-enactments and camps, gathering the signatures of officers, enlisted men, and their ladies.

inspire civilians. During wartime women might feel guilty about the expense and frivolity of fancy work, but making beautiful and creative items to be donated to a fair was a patriotic duty. Civilians could socialize, dine out, shop, and enjoy musical entertainment with the excuse of supporting the cause as they bought their tickets to the latest fundraiser.

While thousands of Fairs busied women North and South, the best documented were the Sanitary Fairs, held under the auspices of the U.S. Sanitary Commission. The first Sanitary Fair was Chicago's Northwestern Fair, organized by Mary Livermore and Elizabeth Hoge in October, 1863. After the hard-fought Union victory at Gettysburg,

Silk was the favored fabric for fashionable clothing and elegant quilts in the Civil War era. The plaid silk basque (the upper portion of a dress) reflects the fashion for Balmorals—plaids made popular by Queen Victoria who was Queen of the Scots as well as of England. Sewing scraps from clothing and fabrics like the watered silk ribbon are the types of materials used in the silk quilts of the time. The diamond quilt from the collection of Terry Clothier Thompson has glass beads stitched to the stars in the corners.

Both the quilt and the basque were constructed by hand but embellished with visible machine stitching. Instead of hiding their machine stitching, Civil War era women were proud of their new and expensive sewing machines.

The basque is lined with a shiny cotton typical of clothing at the time and similar to that on the reverse of the quilt. The date of the quilt is unknown but it looks like a Civil War era piece rather than late Victorian when embroidered seam embellishments were almost a rule on silk quilts.

Federal Rose by Terry Clothier Thompson, Lawrence, Kansas, 1991.

Eagles were popular with quilters throughout the nineteenth century. In this version, Terry has substituted a Peace rose for the arrows of war that the federal eagle usually carries. We can imagine such a quilt being made for a fair.

Livermore and other leaders realized that months and possibly years of war would require thousands and tens of thousands of dollars in supplies. They determined to organize a national Fair, from which they might raise $25,000. President Lincoln sent a letter of commendation and a draft of the Emancipation Proclamation that brought $3,000. "I had some desire to retain the paper, but if it shall contribute to the relief and comfort of the soldiers, that will be better," wrote the President.[55]

Livermore, Hoge and their volunteers raised $100,000 in Chicago, an incredible amount that inspired thirty cities to take Ladies' Fairs to new heights of extravagance. In the last two years of the War women donated over $4 million from national and regional branches of the Commission through these events that were more like international expositions than traditional craft bazaars. New York's, held in April, 1864, was a three-week extravaganza that covered the Union Square area with cattle barns, exhibit halls, and machine sheds.

The Sanitary Commission garnered the bulk of the publicity, but the rival Christian Commission also sponsored Fairs for the benefit of Union soldiers. The Grand Fair of the Ladies' Christian Commission entertained San Francisco in August, 1864. According to the *Daily Alta California*:

"The Hall will be most tastefully decorated with floral wreaths, garlands and National emblems, and a number of the finest paintings and works of art from the private galleries and collections of our wealthy citizens, have been kindly loaned . . . Very many elegant and curious creations from the fair hands that have been employed for weeks past in this labor of love and patriotism, will be on exhibition, and for sale, and very many of the beautiful creators, themselves, will be in attendance for the purpose of making the necessary negotiations relative to the rates of exchange between nick-nacks and gold and greenbacks."[56]

While Fairs were the talk of the Union towns, women in the Confederacy continued fundraising despite their deprivations. The city of Columbia, South Carolina, held what may have been the last Fair for the Confederacy. In January, 1865, the *Daily South Carolinian* carried an advertisement: "The undersigned, under the instructions of the ladies take pleasure in announcing that the BAZAAR will be opened at 7 p.m. on Tuesday, 17th of January in the State House in the city of Columbia. The purpose of this undertaking—the relief of the sick and suffering in 'Homes' and Hospitals and the Navy." Mary Chesnut was living in Columbia; her pessimism is reflected in her dairy entries where she alludes to the Babylonian king who found his doom predicted in an inscription. "Jan 16. The bazaar will be a Belshazzar affair. The handwriting is on the wall. Bad news everywhere . . . Jan 17. Bazaar opens today . . . the last bazaar lags superfluous." Within days Sherman's troops were in Columbia. She fled before the city burned.[57]

Northern Lily and Southern Rose

Northern Lily and Southern Rose by
Terry Clothier Thompson, Lawrence,
Kansas, 1996

This is the kind of fancy quilt that might have been made for a fair. Photographs and descriptions of fairs show appliquéd designs as well as silk pieced quilts, flag quilts, and Log Cabins. Terry Clothier Thompson was inspired to make a quilt for an imaginary Union Fair by some lines of Lucy Larcom, a New England abolitionist and feminist who published a "Call to Kansas" during the Kansas Troubles in 1855. After the Kansas-Nebraska bill mandated that settlers would vote to open the Kanzas Territory (as it was then spelled) to slavery or declare it a free state, partisans from both sides joined emigrants looking for fertile land, and Kansas became a crusade, with battle cries in print, sermon, and song. Larcom's "Call" invited Northern women to "sing upon the Kansas plains the song of liberty."

Sister true, join us too,
Where the Kansas flows;
Let the Northern lily bloom
With the Southern rose.[58]

Larcom's imagery is so quilt-like with its allusions to the two primary appliqué designs, lilies and roses, that Terry decided to adapt a Union shield she'd seen in an 1860s album quilt. Her Union quilt, rather than being strictly partisan, is a call for conciliation between the Northern Lilies and the Southern Roses. The combination of words Union and Liberty echo Daniel Webster's speech in congress in 1850 that set the tone for the North through the years leading up to the War, "Liberty and Union. That... sentiment, dear to every true American heart. Liberty and Union, now and forever, one and inseparable." (For another quilt inspired by Larcom's lines see page 17.)

The block is an old pattern, with names such as Millwheel or Snowball. It is one of the many variations of the Rob Peter to Pay Paul design, which sounds like a good name for a nineteenth-century version of the pattern.

Size: 80½" x 80½"
Rob Peter to Pay Paul Blocks: 8" finished

FABRIC REQUIREMENTS
• Rob Peter to Pay Paul blocks: Terry was thinking 1850s and earlier when she chose the fabrics for the Rob Peter to Pay Paul blocks. She knew she wanted to make them large, so she picked large-scale prints in a variety of florals, stripes, plaids, and pictorials. There are 64 quarter-circle blocks, making 16 scrappy circles. You'll need a total of 4 yards of scraps.
• Center block background: The center is a 32½" square, so you will need a yard of a neutral colored fabric in a good 100% cotton broadcloth (unbleached muslin is not a good choice). Look for a slightly

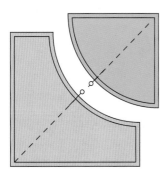

Mark the center with a pin.

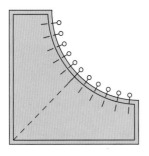

Pin around the curve.

Quarter Circle

off-white or ecru fabric for a period look.

- Setting triangles: The setting triangles surrounding the center square require 1⅝ yards each of a rather flamboyant period print.
- Federal Shield: ¼ yard each of red and blue solids, ⅓ yard of white
- Flowers, Leaves, Stems, and Lettering: The flowers, leaves, stems, and lettering are calico prints. You will need ⅓ yard of red, ½ yard of green, and ¾ yard of yellow-orange (this includes the fabric for the lettering).
- Backing: 4¾ yards
- Binding: ¾ yard (See Binding, page 123.)

CUTTING AND SEWING

Rob Peter to Pay Paul Blocks

To piece the 16 blocks, start by stitching 64 quarter-circles. Make the templates without the seam allowance. Mark around the template with a pencil on the back of the fabrics, adding a quarter-inch seam allowance as you cut. You will then have a line to use as a stitching guide. To find the center of each curve fold the piece in half, fingerpress a crease, and mark with a pin. With right sides together, line up the pins and center creases, re-pin the center, and pin around the curve aligning the pencil lines. Stitch from edge to edge on the pencil lines, easing around the curve. Because this is a large block, the curve is gentle and easy to stitch; there is no need to clip the curve. Press the curve to the large side. Assemble the 64 quarter-circles into 16 blocks. Set aside.

The Center Block

Cut a 32½″ square from the center background fabric. The square will be turned on point. Refer to appliqué instructions on page 73-74 and prepare the appliqué elements. Lay them out on the background following the illustration and photo for placement.

The Federal Shield:

Cut nine red strips and eight white strips 1½″ x 12″ inches. Stitch the strips together with a ¼″ seam allowance, starting and ending with red. Press seams toward the red. Fold the red and white striped yardage in half and mark the center with a pin at the top and the bottom. Set aside. Make a template for the top of the Federal Shield; include the ¼″ seam allowance on the template. Cut the top of the Federal Shield from the solid blue fabric. Mark the center with a pin at the bottom. Match the center pins and stitch the blue top and the red and white yardage together along the edge indicated on the template. To cut out the shield for appliqué, fold in half vertically. Following the slight curve in the Federal Shield top, mark a gentle curve on the red-and-white-striped area to the bottom center pin. Refer to the photo. When you are satisfied with the curve, cut away the excess. After you appliqué the lettering the shield will be appliquéd to the center background fabric.

Appliquéd Letters:

Terry developed this quick way to appliqué words because she wanted to express her sentiments on her quilts. She uses her continuous strip alphabet technique to title quilts and summarize the symbolism in words among the pictures and patterns. At first she cut the strips into parts to construct the letters, but found it time consuming and frustrating (parts always got lost). Then she developed a way to use a continuous strip for each letter, creating small pleats as she turned the corners. Some letters require an extra little strip inserted here and there. For example the middle bar in the letter "E" is an extra strip.

To prepare the strips and make the technique easy, use a bias-strip maker which automatically folds over both raw edges ¼″. They come in several sizes and are available at fabric stores. Terry used the 1″ size for the lettering in *Northern Lily and Southern Rose.*

Rotary cut 1 ½″ strips from the *straight grain* of the fabric. At the tip of each strip cut a point. Set the iron on cotton with no steam (to avoid burning your fingers with steam). Lay the strip down on the ironing board and pin the pointed tip to the cover. Holding the "handle" of the bias tool and the iron in the other hand, slowly and gently pull the maker along the strip, pressing the folded edge as you pull. You may have to coax it through with a pin. If your fabric is resistant to creasing, spray it with a mist of water or spray starch. Wind each pressed strip around a piece of cardboard (not too tightly, but firmly) and pin the end of the strip. The strips will then keep their folds until you are ready for them. You can fold these edges with your fingers and an iron, but it's tricky.

Terry lays out the words on her quilts in an informal, free-hand style. She doesn't worry too much about spacing or uniform size because she likes the liveliness of the "unstructured" word. Begin by pinning the first letter in place. Fold corners to create the pleat. Lay out all the letters in the word to assure they will fit the space. Lay out LIBERTY on the blue top of the Federal Shield, and lay out UNION on the center block background following the photo and quilt diagram. You may baste the letters or just leave the pins in as you sew.

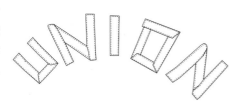

The fastest way to sew the letters down is by machine stitching with a top stitch close to the edge. The idea is to sew a continuous line without stopping—something that takes a little practice. You'll have to backstitch as you turn corners and tuck in the pleats. Terry uses long quilter's pins to keep the edges of the letters turned under and to poke back any edges that pop out as she's sewing. Start sewing on the long side of the letter (not at the short ends) and experiment until the continuous line becomes easier. Of course, you can always hand appliqué or use a running stitch on the top. See *Pea Ridge Lily,* page 104. Stitch in the manner you prefer.

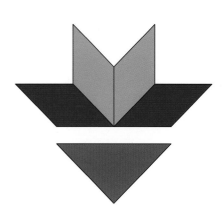

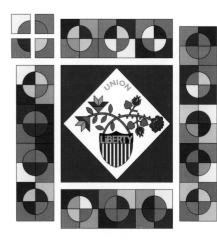

Quilt Top Construction

Setting Triangles

Lilies:

The two lilies are pieced and then appliquéd to the background. Cut templates for the lily petals and calyx. Add dots to stop stitching ¼″ from the edges; they will be turned under when you appliqué the lilies to the background. Stitch four diamonds together, then add the triangular calyx to the bottom. Make two. See the illustration.

Reverse Appliquéd Rose:

The large rose is sewn in the reverse appliqué method that was often used in the nineteenth century. Cut a template for the rose including the lines at the center for the reverse appliqué. Place the template face up on the right side of the rose fabric and mark with a pencil around the outside and just inside the openings in the center of the rose so the pencil lines will not show when appliquéd. Cut out the rose fabric, leaving about 1″ from the outside line all the way around. Later you will re-cut with the smaller seam allowance. Place a 7″ square of yellow-orange fabric under the rose and baste the two together around the outside edges. To reverse appliqué the center of the rose, cut on the dotted line about ½″, fold under small sections, and appliqué, then cut again and appliqué until all the slits in the center are appliquéd to the yellow-orange square. You will have a small seam allowance. Take care as you get to the corners not to cut into the corner too deeply. Match the color of the thread to the rose. Carefully cut away the excess yellow-orange fabric from the back of the rose, leaving a ¼″ beyond your appliqué stitches. Re-cut the outside edge of the rose to the seam allowance you are comfortable with for appliqué, from ³⁄₁₆″ to ¼″. Your rose is now ready to appliqué to the center block.

Leaves, Stems, and Rosebuds:

Cut templates for the lily leaves, rose leaves, thorns, rosebuds, and bud stems. Place the template face up on the right side of the fabric and cut out, adding the seam allowance you prefer for appliqué. There are six lily leaves, three rose leaves, seven rose thorns, two rosebuds, and two bud stems. Prepare two bias strips 1½″ x 22″ for the long stems. Pin all the elements onto the center block, following the quilt diagram and photo for placement. Appliqué using the technique of your choice.

Setting Triangles:

The four setting triangles are cut from two 26⅜″ squares. The squares are cut in half diagonally. The straight of grain will be on the outside edges. Find the center of each side of the center square and the long side of the triangles. Pin to mark the centers. Match the centers and stitch the triangles on, chasing them around the square, as carpenter's say. The center square will float about 1″ from the edge of the triangles, which avoids cutting off the points of the center block.

Pieced Borders

Stitch three of the Rob Peter to Pay Paul blocks together and add to the top of the center square. Repeat for the bottom. Stitch two rows of five

Rob Peter to Pay Paul blocks together and add to the sides. Note: You may need to trim equally the outside edges of the center block unit to be the same measurement as the three Rob Peter to Pay Paul blocks sewn together.

Quilting

Use a utility pattern for the Rob Peter to Pay Paul border. For the center you might want to do a nineteenth-century type of utility design; for example, parallel diagonal lines in groups of three. They used to quilt right over their appliqué, something we rarely do. If you'd rather bring a twentieth-century sensibility to your quilting in the center you might quilt some fancy designs in the spaces and do several rows of outline quilting around the appliquéd flowers. See Utility Quilting beginning on page 122.

For tips on batting and binding see the General Instructions beginning on page 122.

Tips for Reproduction Fabrics

Mary Madden's album (page 10) is sashed with a reproduction purple calico, one from Marcus Brothers designer Judie Rothermel, whose reproduction lines are among the most authentic. Purple was a difficult color to obtain with natural dyes on cotton. I am guessing that most of the mid-nineteenth-century purples were dyed with logwood. They were never intense, but usually a flat lavender. Many purples were quite fugitive, fading over time to a dull brown. But others survived well in their original intensities.

Look for prints with purple backgrounds. You want lavenders rather than blue-violets, magentas, or orchids. The prints can be small or medium sized, but the figures should be dark. On the originals the figures were often a darker shade of purple, but in the reproductions the figures are usually black. A little white showing through as a figure is also typical of the time.

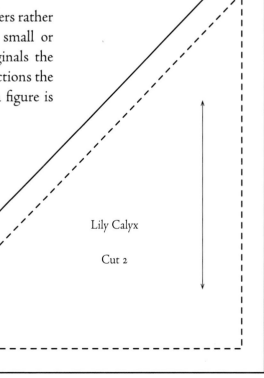

Lily Calyx

Cut 2

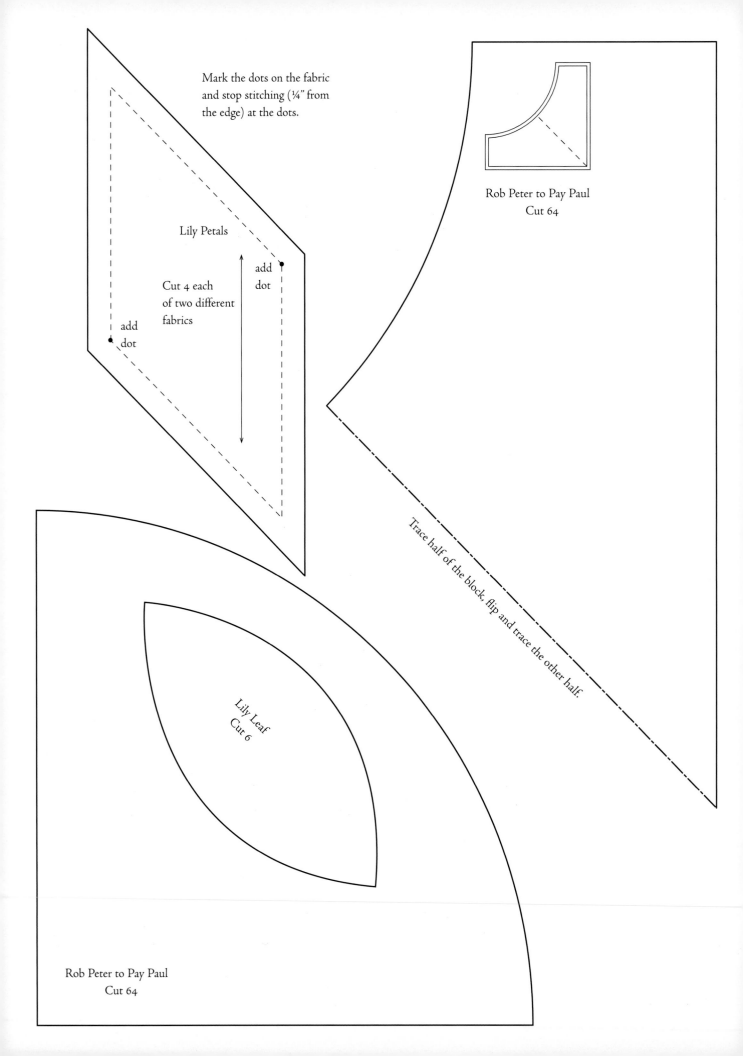

Mark the dots on the fabric and stop stitching (¼" from the edge) at the dots.

Rob Peter to Pay Paul
Cut 64

Lily Petals

add dot

add dot

Cut 4 each of two different fabrics

Trace half of the block, flip and trace the other half.

Lily Leaf
Cut 6

Rob Peter to Pay Paul
Cut 64

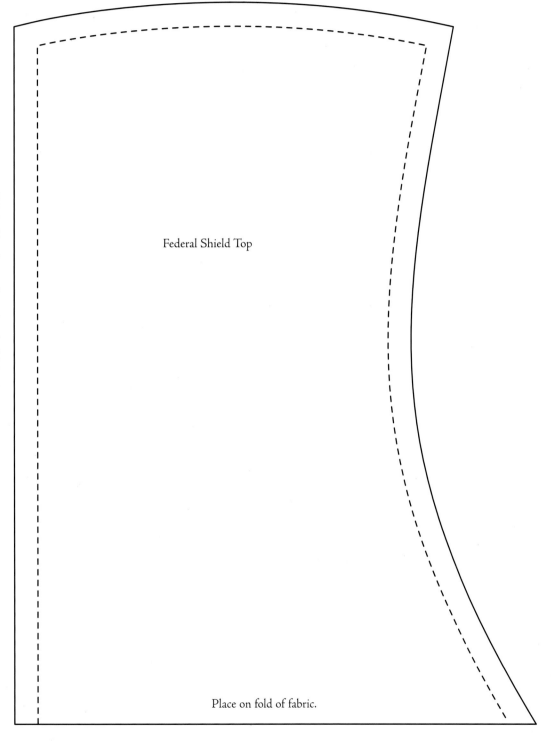

Stitch this edge to the red and white strips.

Federal Shield Top

Place on fold of fabric.

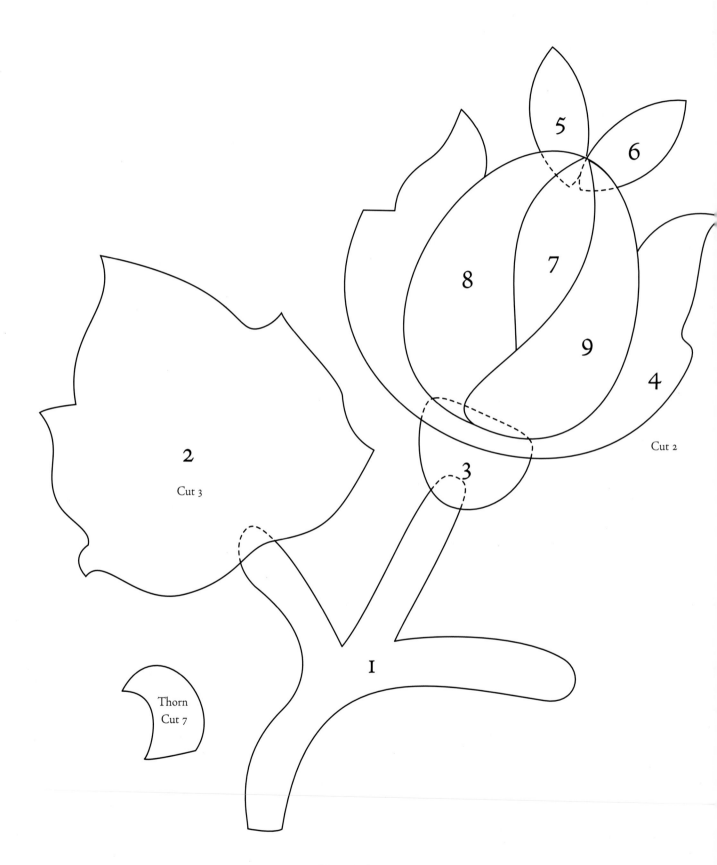

5

6

8

7

9

4

Cut 2

2

Cut 3

3

1

Thorn
Cut 7

Rose Leaves, Stem, and Rose Buds

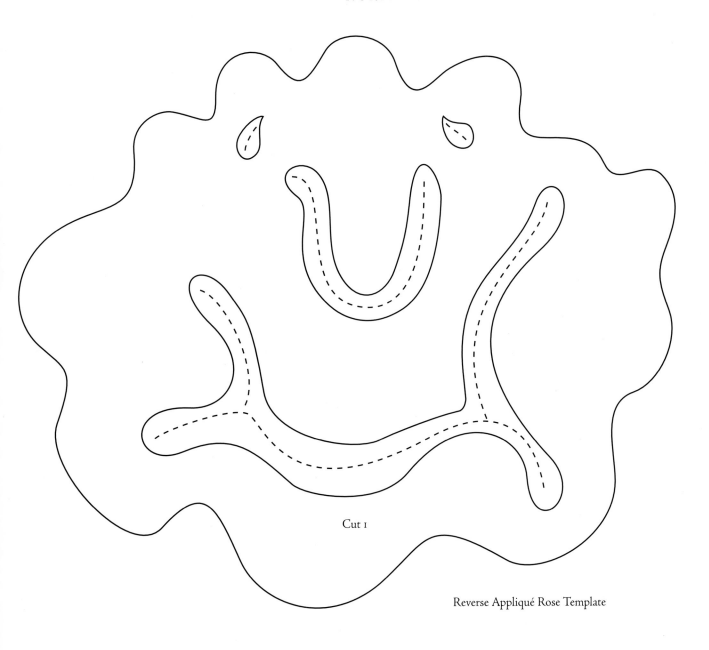

Cut 1

Reverse Appliqué Rose Template

CHAPTER 6

"In War Time,"
Hardship, Homespun,
and Linsey

"Times are hard but I do not think we ought to complain. . . . I have been wearing homespun dresses this winter to save my calico and knit my stockings to keep my bought ones for summer."

Mary Byson, Texas, 1864

Reading the War News from *Peterson's Magazine*, April, 1862

The war that was to shed just a thimble full of blood killed thousands upon thousands of men. From April, 1861, to April, 1865, women waited for news of their husbands, fathers, sons, brothers, and friends. Mary Chesnut captured their four years of war weariness when she wrote, "Battle after battle—disaster after disaster. Every morning's paper enough to kill a well woman or age a strong and hearty one."[59]

Sarah Morgan lost two of her brothers in a week during the last winter. It took a month after she learned of their deaths before she could bring herself to comment in her diary. "We cannot remember the day when our brothers were not all in all to us. What the boys would think; what the boys would say; what we would do when the boys came home, that has been our sole thought through life. A life time's hope wrecked in a moment—God help us!"[60]

In War Time, by Jane A. Blakely Stickle, Shaftsbury, Vermont, 1863, 80˝ x 80˝, Collection of the Bennington Museum, Bennington, Vermont. Photo courtesy of the Museum. Jane Stickle was 50 years old when she finished this extraordinary sampler.

81

By that last year Emma Holmes was resigned to loss. She signed to her diary, "During the last month what a long roll of death have I to record among friends & acquaintances—some on the battle field, others from wounds, & others again falling from the sickle of the Great Reaper, borne down by disease."[61]

Jane A. Stickle made a quilt (page 80) in Vermont that seems to reflect her wait during the War. Her sampler of 225 patterns and 5,602 pieces speaks to us about the day-in—day-out anxieties of living through a war. Her signature is simple, yet speaks volumes; she signed her name, counted the number of pieces, and wrote the words "In War Time, 1863." We can marvel at the beauty and sheer number of blocks and pieces, and imagine her using her patchwork, a repetitive, sometimes obsessive, task to keep her mind at peace. Perhaps a quilt as complex as this one could only have been made "In War Time."[62]

Quilts marking the days of the four-year War seem to be a product only of the North. Although Southern women write about making quilts, we find very few surviving Confederate quilts. Before the War, quiltmaking thrived in parts of the South. After the War, quiltmaking continued despite an association with poverty and wartime deprivations.

Detail of *Jackson Star*, by Ellen R. Eastman Wilson (1845-1927), Cedar Point, Iowa, 1862, 73 1/2″ x 76″, Collection of Jeananne Wright, Longmont, Colorado.

Ellen Eastman was 17 years old and teaching at a country school in Linn County when she passed her wartime recesses by piecing this quilt. (Note that it is machine quilted.) Her story is typed on a note stitched to the front of the quilt. We might call this pattern Feathered Star, but the note says it is Jackson Star, probably named for President Andrew Jackson. The Illinois Quilt Project uncovered another Jackson Star with the name pieced into the design. This name, so foreign to us, gives us some clue as to how little we know about quilt pattern names during the mid-nineteenth century. How many other quilt patterns carried political names that are long forgotten?

By 1862 quilts were already dropping in status, according to Lou Burge, whose mother Dolly Lunt Burge quoted her: "Lou is making a bed quilt but she says she is never going to cut up peices (sic) again for such work, that only poor white folks make bed quilts, that the rich buy blankets."[63]

Northerner Caroline Seabury, living behind Confederate lines in Mississippi during the early years of the war, also held quiltmaking in contempt. "Almost for the first time in my life—this summer time hangs heavily on my hands for lack of something to busy both mind and body. With nothing to sew because there is not material to be had, except as now & then a call is made for soldier's clothes. Even after learning to twist on a 'great wheel' there is nothing left to twist—A new book I have not seen in two years, nor even heard what has been published in Yankee land—nothing has been here. Believing fully in the old maxim, 'Satan finds some mischief for idle hands to do,' & fearing I might illustrate its truth, I have been reduced to the last semblance of occupation—patchwork—in company with my friends here—a last resort in the hour of extremity." [64]

Quiltmaking may have fallen out of fashion with these young women, but it was not a drop in status that caused the absence of Confederate quilts. Rather it was a desperate lack of fabric. Many view quilts as a product of scarcity and conclude that patchwork bedding would be common where fabric is hard to obtain. In reality, patchwork requires an abundance of fabric and quilting an abundance of thread. Within months of Fort Sumter both became scarce in the would-be country of the Confederacy, which had little industrial capability for producing textiles. Their silks, wools, linens, and cottons, everything down to their pins and needles, were imported by boat from France, Scotland and England, Massachusetts, and New Hampshire. [65]

High prices were caused by a combination of scarcity and inflation; the dollars were Confederate money, banknotes so worthless, Cornelia Peake McDonald complained, that "$200 was required to buy a calico dress." [about ten yards.] Twenty dollars a yard for calico that had a pre-War price of twenty cents seems to be the highest price recorded at the time, but in memoirs written after the War the price went higher. Virginia Clay-Clopton remembered in her autobiography that "Calico of the commonest in those days was sold at twenty-five dollars a yard." [66]

As money lost all value, women measured their wealth in terms of yardgoods and clothing. During the last year of the war Emma Holmes had lost everything; she took a job as teacher for $60 to $80 for the school year, "enough to buy me a calico [dress], a muslin [dress] & a pair of shoes—nine months labor. Well, it is better than nothing." Mary Chesnut, rich enough to wear silk through much of the war, sold her dresses to a used clothing shop in Columbia in 1864. "What a scene—such piles of rubbish—and mixed up with it all, such splendid Parisian silks and satins." A year later, hiding in North Carolina in the month before Appomatox, she and her slave Ellen lived on a barter system, trading yarn for food. "Yarn is our circulating medium. It is the current coin of the realm. . . . I bought five dozen eggs with [yarn] from a wagon.

Unknown child. Girls wore short, full skirts and off-the-shoulder sleeves. The fabric in her dress may be silk or cotton, but it is probably delaine, a wool/cotton combination fabric.

The child's dress and the child's quilt, made by a member of the Burkhart family in Illinois, 1855-1875, are of the light wools so popular for clothing during the War. The delaine dress is from the collection of Terry Thompson; the delaine quilt, a simplified version of the Log Cabin, is owned by Barbara and Kern Jackson. For a photograph and instructions for this quilt see the project instructions beginning on page 115.

Eggs for Lent. And to show that I have faith in humanity, I paid her in advance—in yarn for something to eat, which she promises to bring tomorrow."[67]

Factory-spun sewing thread became so hard to find that women abandoned their sewing machines to sew again by hand because machines used too much thread. Lucy Chase, a Northern relief worker living on Craney Island, Virginia, remarked often in her letters home about the lack of basic sewing necessities for the hundreds of former slaves who sought refuge on this Union-held island in a Confederate state. "We feel irresistibly impelled to work early, and late, until every refugee upon the Island has tasted one day of comfort, at least, in the shape of clothes. . . . We have already distributed the large quantity of valuable material which came from Phil[adelph]ia, and it is, even now, warming those it was sent to bless. . . . We have not yet found one woman who cannot sew." But Chase had little to offer the women who were willing to make their own clothes. "A quarter of a spool of cotton, one needle; and two pins! to a full grown woman!"[68]

Catherine Edmonston's brother-in-law sent her a welcome gift of stationery, envelopes, pens, "and what I consider as a present indeed. Four papers of English pins! I told him if he dared to send me Yankee pins I would make a cushion of him & I see he has heeded." Virginia

Clay-Clopton recalled her deprivations. "Needles were becoming precious as heirlooms; pins were the rarest of luxuries. For the greater part of the time locust thorns served us instead." Although the needle-like thorns of the locust tree might substitute for pins, there was no substitute for factory-made needles.[69]

Unknown woman. Her hair parted in the middle and pulled back with a fullness at the side is typical of the Civil War era, as is her dress.

The rules for fashion were rigid. The waist fell at the natural waist or a little higher, sleeves were full at the elbow and skirts were gathered evenly all the way around, over wide hoops. A jewel neckline with a small lace collar is also typical, as is the dress made of one fabric. Only young women would wear a skirt of one fabric and a waist of another. The fashion emphasized a horizontal, broad look, quite a contrast to the lithe, vertical look we value today. Too many re-enactors look at a photo like this and assume the dress is a cotton print, but the fabric is likely wool or silk or a combination fabric.

Hexagonal Log Cabin, unknown maker, 1860-1880, Collection of the author

This unusual, intricate variation of the Log Cabin pattern may have been made years after the War but many of the wool and silk fabrics are typical of the 1860s. The backing is a green and blue plaid, a light wool of the kind of fabric that might have made a Balmoral skirt.

Union troops knew the value of sewing and knitting supplies. General Benjamin Butler, generally called "Beast" Butler for his disrespect to the women of occupied New Orleans, banned knitting needles in the city. He knew the women sitting on their piazzas, needles clacking as they glared at his soldiers marching by, were knitting socks for Confederates. When Yankees rampaged through the Morgan house in Baton Rouge they stole one sewing machine and damaged the other. "As mother's was too heavy to move, they merely smashed the needles," wrote Sarah Morgan.[70]

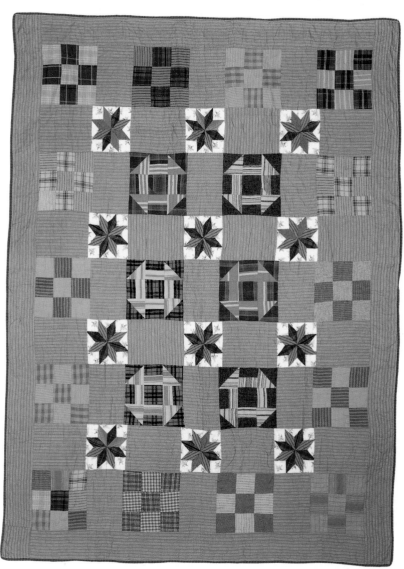

Sherman's March by Terry Clothier Thompson, Lawrence, Kansas, 1996

The nine-patch in the center of this flannel quilt by Terry Clothier Thompson is a common pattern with an uncommon number of names. We know it best as Churn Dash or Monkey Wrench, but it's also called Sherman's March and Lincoln's Platform[71]. When Terry decided to make a warm quilt "just for herself," she remembered the look of the Southern linsey quilts. She pieced simple designs that would have been around during the Civil War and featured Sherman's March, in honor of all the women who suffered the hardships of living in the paths of the soldiers. She chose plaids, checks and stripes in the browns and reds that reminded her of the dyes found in linseys and jeans cloth. Today's cotton flannels, machine spun, factory-dyed and factory woven, are a homey substitute for the truly home-woven fabrics made during the War.

General William Sherman's troops may be remembered for their slash-and-burn warfare as they marched through Georgia and the Carolinas, but some soldiers brought gifts, hoping to win female loyalties. Mrs. Campbell Bryce remembered the occupation of Columbia, South Carolina, when two Union soldiers barged into her house "smoking, though otherwise respectful. One of them came up to me with a handful of spool cotton and papers of needles. Though they were worth their weight in gold to us at that time, I refused them; I could not take them from his hand." Bryce's action reduces Confederate pride to a minute level, a sliver of sharp steel. Pride was the price of a needle, and she would not barter.[72]

Whether the price of calico was 20 cents or $20, few Southerners could afford factory-made fabric. After a year or two of war, most women learned to do without. "I have not a spare blanket or comforter left, and we mend our clothes nicely to keep from buying new supplies, which are sold at such high rates," Lucy Virginia Smith French of McMinnville, Tennessee, wrote in her diary in 1862. "Calicos, Domestics, and Linseys, etc. are at ruinous prices and we are endeavoring to 'Make out' with what we have until the 'blockade' is opened." The Domestics to which she referred were inexpensive white and unbleached cottons from American mills, hence the name domestic. Today we call similar cloth muslin. Among its many other uses in the nineteenth century, domestic cloth, like muslin in the twentieth, was used to back quilts.[73]

Linseys were a combination fabric with a warp of cotton and weft of wool. Decades earlier, linsey-woolsey had been, as the name implies, a combination linen and wool fabric. By mid-century cotton substituted for the linen warp. Despite the fact that most of it was a cotton/wool combination, people continued to call it linsey-woolsey or just linsey. The coarse cloth was often woven at home, of homespun wool and factory-spun cotton yarns. Before the War linsey could be purchased; it was spun and woven in textile mills as well as in cottage industries with a loom or two.

Because it combines two fibers that are dyed at the yarn stage, linsey cloth is always two colors, commonly blue wool and white cotton, or two shades of red or brown. Much linsey was a simple jeans fabric, a grid of two colors in either a plain weave or twill weave much like our blue jeans today. Checks, plaids, and stripes made good use of the two-color yarns.

Linsey cloth may have been the homespun that Mrs. Mark Valentine of Richmond remembered "We had an aunt in the country, and she managed to raise a few sheep. From them she gathered wool and spun it into cloth and gave my sister and myself each a dress, which we made and wore with great pride over big hoop skirts, and were the envy of all our girl friends."[74]

The Richmond belles envied only her patriotism, because linsey or woolen homespun had never been considered comfortable, fashionable, or flattering. Yet due to its plainness, homespun became a symbol of Southern pride, a defiant response to the Yankee embargo. Caroline Seabury, trying to find her way North by posing as a Southerner, encountered a family clad in homespun on the road to Vicksburg. "They showed me cloths they had spun and woven for themselves—saying 'I'll wear homespun as long as I live before I'd depend on the Yankees for it—wouldn't you?' Of course I said I would."[75]

Such patriotic pride was advocated in the popular culture of the time. Poems lauded homespun, and a popular song of the day was *The Homespun Dress* by Carrie Bell Sinclair, set to the tune of the Southern anthem *The Bonnie Blue Flag*.

" *Hurrah! Hurrah!*
For the sunny South so dear;
Three cheers for the homespun dress
The Southern ladies wear."

Necessity forced urban and coastal women to take up the coarse fabrics of their rural sisters. But these women, who had purchased manufactured cloth for decades, had no skills in spinning and weaving. Their mothers and grandmothers may have spent hours at great wheels and looms producing yards of linen and wool, but by the 1840s cotton cloth produced by New England mills was cheap enough and available enough to make spinning and weaving forgotten arts, except in backwaters and on large plantations where slave labor was cheap. The blockade forced white women to relearn the skills, sometimes from their slaves. And new talents became a point of pride.

Emma Holmes, on a Christmas visit in 1863, found young friends showing them off. "Blanche cannot be more than ten, and one morning her father told her to try and see how much she could do in one day. She carded till breakfast and, between then and dinner, spun three fine cuts." [76]

Tryphena Blanche Fox, a small-scale slave holder, wrote her mother in the North that she was "reduced to homespun dress and unbleached domestic underclothes, but I am contented; I have learned to realize that if one is warm and neatly dressed it is all sufficient . . . I little thought three years ago that I should be wearing coarse unbleached now. I have found it uncomfortably warm, but the past few mornings have been cool and I did not mind it; it is just such as I used to give my servants . . . Northern people must not think we are most starved out or naked—everybody is making homespun." [77]

In the decades before the War, the cloth was not only the clothing of rustic whites; it was the fabric that branded a black a slave. Northern abolitionists might have enjoyed the irony of driving the plantation class to adopt the same clothing as their slaves. What slaves wore before the War varied according to where they lived, what kind of crops the plantation raised, and the attitude of the woman who managed the household sewing.

Homespinning, of course, required raw materials: cotton, wool, and linen. As the War and the blockade dragged on, raw materials became scarce. Women took new pride in using scraps and salvaged fibers. Emma Holmes wrote of her Aunt Mary's ingenuity in making "Oliver, her little negro boy about twelve years old, whom she taught to work on

Linsey Quilt, maker unknown, last half of the nineteenth century, Collection of Merikay Waldvogel. Photo by Terry Wild Studio. This simple quilt is made of a variety of home-woven fabrics of cotton and wool.

the sewing machine and make all kinds of garments on it, as well as to spin—go every day to the depot and pick up the loose cotton lying about and spin it—then ravel and card up scraps of red flannel and other woolen which he also spun. Then she paid a woman ten cents a yard to weave it and made 14 yards of stout warm cloth—enough to clothe him for a year—and at a cost of $1.40 and some trouble and perseverance." Oliver received no credit; his skills, trouble, and perseverance were taken for granted.[78]

Cornelia Peake McDonald recalled her desperate recycling efforts to dress her children for the last winter of the War. "I had ripped up a cotton mattress and had it carded and spun, had dyed one half brown with walnut hulls, and left the other white. Out of this a very neat check was made which clothed Kenneth and the three little boys."[79]

Homespun and the hardships that dictated its manufacture became part of the Southern memory of the War. The cloth was so durable that for the fortunate the plaids, checks, and jeans cloth outlasted the need for subsistence clothing. Some of that homespun was cut into patchwork for post-War quilts and comforters. These rough and simple quilts were made for several reasons. They served as blankets in post-War poverty. They also satisfied the practical nature of quiltmakers who couldn't throw such durable cloth away. And many quilts were made to preserve the memories of homespun days, as one family with roots in Missouri told the researchers in the Kansas quilt project. Although many quilts of homespun linseys and woolens were probably made, we

This whole-cloth quilt of wool is probably home-spun, home-dyed, and home-woven. Last half of the nineteenth century. Collection of Terry Clothier Thompson.

This coarse quilt is reversible, one side a check of madder red and indigo blue wool yarns; the other a twill weave of the same two colors, a jeans fabric. The bias binding is a brown factory-woven cotton. The quilt was found in Kansas, but was probably made in an Eastern or Southern state. Kansas, a Union state, was settled after factory-made cottons were cheap and available and home-spinning and weaving was no longer necessary. Although some Kansans complained of a fabric shortage during the War, few had the skills, equipment, or raw material to produce fabric at home.

rarely find them. Merikay Waldvogel, a Tennessee quilt historian who has studied quilts of homespun, believes that many of those she sees were made after the War as memories of the Lost Cause. Over the generations the memories have been forgotten, and the rough comforters are too often dismissed as fit only for furniture padding or animal bedding. Waldvogel continues to call our attention to these unrecognized souvenirs of the War. In the Tennessee quilt search, she and co-director Bets Ramsey found a pillow of crazy patchwork cut from checks, plaids, and gray cloth made by Mary High Prince in 1910. Upon it an embroidered poem recalls Carrie Bell Sinclair's proud song with an echo of grief:

"Hoorah for the home spun
dresses we southern ladies
wore in time of the war.
Every piece here,
Sad memories it brings
back to me.
For our hearts were weary and restless.
And our life was full of care,
The burden laid up on us
seemed greater than
we could bear."

Mary Prince 1910, age 70 yrs.[80]

CHAPTER 7

"It Didn't Look Like a Yankee Person Could Be So Mean" Quilts Buried with the Silver

"I have two quilts that were buried during the Confederate War. My mother made them in 1857. One is the Open Rose. The other is the Album quilt with the names of friends on it. They're good now! The Open Rose was a great quilt and the Rose and Bud . . . I've seen the Yankees come and burn down the houses. I saw two large houses burned to the ground. When they came to our house, I went out and sat in the Captain's lap and begged him not to burn our house. I was six years old. I hugged and kissed him and begged him not to burn our house. My mother was a widow. They didn't burn it."

Interview with Lula Bowers, Luray, South Carolina, 1938[81]

Union sympathizers driven from their homes during the Battle of Pea Ridge, Arkansas. Notice the man on the lower right huddled in a nine-patch quilt. Sketch from *Frank Leslie's Illustrated.*

Citizens of Atlanta fleeing before Sherman's Army. How many quilts were bundled with other valuables? From *Frank Leslie's Illustrated.*

Calico Flag, a faithful copy of one made by Palmyra Mitchell, Sharon Durken Rush, Glencoe, Minnesota, 1996

Lula Bowers's memory of Sherman's March through South Carolina includes one of the common stories about the War. Tales of quilts hidden to keep them from marauding Yankees is a myth rooted in the truth of events described in diaries and letters. The Confederates suffered the most from marauding troops, so it is in the South that the majority of the tales of buried quilts are told. Yet an occasional Northern quilt survives with a story that it was hidden from Southern soldiers. The Illinois Quilt Project found a Mexican Rose appliqué quilt that was buried in Indiana by Sarah Herron Hinds and her husband. They were terrified of Confederate raider John Hunt Morgan and his men, who swept up from Kentucky in the summers of 1862 and 1863. Like many a quilt supposedly buried and retrieved, the piece is covered with stains. Quilts acquire stains in many ways, and at least some of the tales told about stained quilts are probably exaggerations. Illinois Quilt Project authors Duane and Rachel Elbert view the water spots as battle scars, an analogy that helps to explain why so many quilts survive with the same story. "For more than 125 years, this Civil War survivor has proudly borne its battle scars and, as a firsthand witness, the quilt has offered each new owner a personal contact with an American tragedy."[82]

Palmyra Mitchell of Union Mills, Missouri, held Confederate sentiments in a state occupied by Union troops. She was in her late twenties during the War, married to miller John W. Mitchell, a Kentuckian. Her family recalled the story she had told them about the day a group of Union soldiers rode up to her farm and demanded to see a Union flag. When the Mitchells explained they had none, they were told to find a flag soon—the soldiers would be back. If no flag flew, the house would be burned. Palmyra ran to her scrap bag and found enough red, white, and blue fabric to make a small flag. She quickly pieced thirteen stripes of Turkey red calico and white. On a patch of blue cotton she appliquéd a large white star surrounded by thirteen smaller stars.

She repeated the blue field and stars on the back so the flag was reversible. On the side—the edge with the stripes and not the stars—she added two loops for hanging.

When the Union soldiers returned, the Mitchells were displaying the proper flag and their home was spared. The loops indicate that they flew it upside down with the stars at the bottom, but the Army seems not to have noticed her small rebellion.

The flag was passed down in the family, and in recent years descendants gave it to Missouri's Weston Historical Museum where it is on display. Although the Turkey red is still bright, the figures in the red calico are rotting away, making the little flag extremely fragile. One way to conserve such fragile textiles is to copy them as Sharon Rush has done in her 1996 copy (page 92).

While guerilla tactics like Morgan's raids were common throughout the war, General William Tecumseh Sherman carried the idea of warring against civilians into a formal battle strategy. Sherman's tactic of sending an army on an extended march across enemy territory began in November, 1864, when he sent 62,000 men to march from Chattanooga southeast across Georgia to Savannah and then back up the Carolina coast. He expected the troops to march fifteen miles a day, and he gave them no supply trains. In his order he directed the army: "Forage liberally on the country during the march. In districts and neighborhoods where the army is unmolested, no destruction of . . . property should be permitted; but should guerrillas or bushwhackers molest our march. . . or otherwise manifest local hostility, the army commanders should order and enforce a devastation more or less relentless according to the measure of such hostility."[83]

Tintype of an unknown woman in a Paisley shawl

The "pocket" in the center of the picture is a reproduction by Terry Clothier Thompson, of the type of bag women wore under their dresses to hold their keys, sewing, and household necessities. Here it represents the "running bag" that diarist Sarah Morgan described often in her years as a Confederate refugee. She kept the bag packed and often went to bed with a clean dress and traveling clothes laid out, in case she was awakened during the night with news of advancing Union armies. She might have carried in her hoops a bag with her best laces and some four-patch blocks she was sewing, her autograph album, and *cartes-de-visites* and tintype photos of her family and friends. The warm quilted bonnet is a silk Shaker, quite the thing at the time. The shawl is a wool Paisley, convenient fashion for a woman on the run.

Pea Ridge Lily by a member of the Pope Family, Benton County, Arkansas, about 1860, Collection of Jeananne Wright, 67″ x 77″

When Jeananne bought this quilt in Denver she was told that the Pope family knew a battle was coming in northwest Arkansas in March, 1862. They buried the quilt with other valuables in a wooden box or trunk to save them from the Union soldiers. Many family members died in the Battle of Pea Ridge, and the story has been handed down with the stained quilt, still bearing its battle scars. For a photograph and instructions for this quilt see the project instructions beginning on page 104.

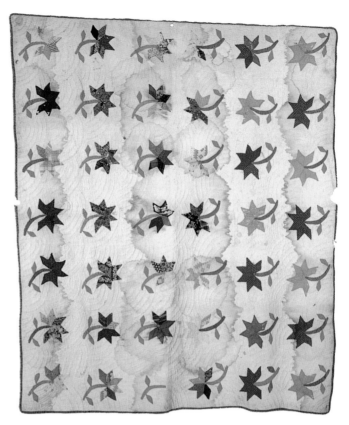

The relentless devastation by soldiers who were hungry, drunk, and furiously revengeful became an American legend. "They say no living thing is found in Sherman's track—only chimneys, like telegraph poles to carry the news of Sherman's army backward," wrote Mary Chesnut. His troops cut an eight-mile swath, with traces still visible today.[84]

Word of Yankee advances terrified women, who feared for their virtue and their lives, but also their silver. Tryphena Blanche Fox of Louisiana wrote her mother shortly after the war: "I prized my silver highly. . . . I had carried it on my person or in my hands carefully done up in a box, everywhere we went, through the war—we saved it from the Yankees, while at Pa's by burying it." Sarah E. Watkins wrote her daughter in a similar vein: "A Yankee raid passed through Winona [Mississippi] last summer. . . . I was very uneasy of fearing they would come here. I buried my silver, my money and my watch. It ruined my watch."[85]

Although white women's panic about their physical safety was generally unecessary, worries about material posessions were wise for both black and white families in the path of the soldiers. The armies took anything that could be eaten, drunk, ridden, worn, or slept under. Soldiers stripped beds, from the big house to the slave cabins. Women often directed their servants to bury their quilts with the silver. The sentimental value of the quilts was probably as important as their functional value as padding for the silver, to prevent scratching and denting.

The Jones/Robarts family of Georgia lived in Sherman's path. Their letters provide a vivid account of the terror from the vengeful Yankees. Mary E. Robarts of Marietta wrote her cousin Mary Jones in May, 1864: "The army is now on this side of the Etowah River. The families from above are fleeing before the enemy. . . . Mr Rogers came down with his laborers & wagons from the ironworks, took up some of Mr. Ardi's valuables & one trunk for us (containing our quilts and silver) and took them to Atlanta."[86]

Mary Jones Mallard wrote her mother from Atlanta about a friend's experiences:

"The Yankees had ripped up their beds, scattered the feathers and carried off the ticking, blankets, and coverings of every description and had burned her own and her children's clothing. And the Union men had killed their cattle. All their provisions had been taken from them, so they were compelled to find another country. Whenever the Yankee officers were remonstrated with for burning and destroying property which was valuable only to the owners, their universal reply was: 'I am sorry for you, but must obey orders.'"[87]

Many first-person accounts tell us of the items packed into trunks to be hidden from enemy raiders. Photographs, diaries, lace, and family silver might be wrapped in the best quilts, like this gorgeous chintz piece from the Fitzsimmons family. Collection of Barbara and Kern Jackson.

Ex-slave Nancy Johnson's testimony was recorded after the War as she and her husband tried to recover $514.50 from the victorious Union, compensation for their horses, hogs, and provisions. They were awarded $155. Her words reveal how much more she lost. "This property all belonged to me and my husband. None of it belonged to Mr. Baggs. I swore to the men so, but they wouldn't believe I could have such things. My girl had a changable silk dress . . . & they took them all—It didn't look like a Yankee person could be so mean. . . . They said we ought not to care what they took for we would get it all back again. . . . come & go along with us; but I wouldn't go because the old man had my youngest child hid away in Tatnal Co: he took her away because she knew where the gold was hid & he didn't want her to tell. My boy was sent out to the swamp to watch the wagons of provisions & the [Union] soldiers took the wagons & the boy, & I never saw him anymore. He was 14 yrs. old. I could have got the child back, but I was afraid my master would kill him. . . . The Lord forgive them for the way they have treated me. The child could not help them from taking the horses. He said that Henry (my boy) halooed for the sake of having the Yankees find him; but the Yankees asked him where he was going & he didn't know they were soldiers & he told them that he was going to Master's mules."[88]

Johnson's testimony informs us not only that many slaves owned property, but also that the soldiers treated master and slave alike. During the 1930s ex-slave Sam Word recalled that a Yankee stole a quilt from his mother. She retaliated, "Why you nasty, stinking rascal. You say you come down here to fight for the negroes, and now you're stealing from them." The soldier replied, "You're a goddamned liar, I'm fighting for $14 a month and the Union."[89]

Soldiers gave many reasons for their behavior, from following orders to mean revenge, but the true motive was often greed compounded by a desire for a souvenir. Rachel Cormany received a Christmas present from her husband in early 1865. "Sat evening Mr. Allison brought me a small package which John Hassen brought from Mr. Cormany to me. I opened in their presence—it contained an oldfashioned tea box in which were packed two beautiful china tea-cups & two odd shaped stone ware cups one stone ware saucer & a china saucer—rebel relics— Nice keep sakes. He is ever thoughtful & kind."[90]

Rachel wouldn't have written of him so sweetly had she been able to read his diary account for that Christmas. "Via Lees Mill to William Gees. . . Made the acquaintance of Miss Rosa Roder, an inveterate little Rebel—and bewitchingly beautiful—but withall exceedingly interesting socially. As relics I got a fine brass candlestick—a steel & Tumbler at Gees . . . I sent Pet, by Hasson—a box with "Relics.""[91]

Quilts also became relics. The Kansas Museum of History owns a beautiful chintz album that is a War souvenir. George Holyoke of the 45th Illinois Volunteer Infantry found it covering another Union soldier in an army camp in the deep South. Realizing its value and fragility, Holyoke bought it to send home to his wife. After the War, he became a minister in Kansas. In 1924 his widow offered the quilt to the state society. At that time the organization collected books and papers, but they agreed to take this quilt, the first in their collection, because of its connection to the Civil War.[92]

The North Carolina Quilt Project recorded the family history of the "War Quilt" in the Cooper family. Dr. Robert Wilkerson Cooper was a lieutenant in a North Carolina regiment of the Confederate Army. While working with the wounded after a battle he found a dead mule with a saddle blanket made from a folded quilt. Again the quilt

Detail of *Blue and Gray Battle Quilt* by Nancy A. Hornback, Wichita, Kansas, 1996. For a photograph and instructions for this quilt see the project instructions beginning on page 35.

Cut-out Chintz Album Quilt, makers unknown, 1840-1860, Collection of the Kansas Museum of History. Photo courtesy of the Kansas Museum of History.

Quilts like this beautiful piece were made along the eastern coast from New Jersey south into the Carolinas. It was probably stolen by a Union soldier, and eventually found its way into the hands of George Holyoke, a soldier from Illinois, who sent it to his wife. Mrs. Holyoke hoped someday to find the original Southern owners, but never did so. In 1924 she donated the quilt to the Kansas State Historical Society. The blocks, each cut of designs from different chintz prints, are signed by many people, mostly from the Mellichamp family.

was an elegant chintz spread, possibly something familiar to him, as these were the quilts made in well-to-do Carolina homes before the war. He took the coverlet to his mother, who washed and mended it and established a tradition that the quilt be used only for special guests.[93]

Both these stories tell us of honorable men who stumbled across a valuable quilt. Few families pass down the more unpleasant tale of great-grandfather stealing civilian bedding, yet quilts and comforters acquired through pillage and plunder must survive in Northern and Southern homes. There must have been thousands of them. So many diarists and letter writers recorded their losses as refugee Sarah Morgan did: "If we could only get home . . . But if we get home, what will we do for bedding? The Yankees did not leave us a single comfort, and only two old bars [mosquito nets] and a pair of ragged sheets, which articles are not to be replaced at any price in the Confederacy, so we must go without. How glad I am that we gave all our blankets to our soldiers last summer! So much saved from the Yankees!"[94]

Order No. 11

Order No. 11 by Terry Clothier
Thompson, Lawrence, Kansas, 1996

The greatest civilian massacre during the Civil War was the sack of my home town, Lawrence, Kansas, in August, 1863. Lawrence symbolized free-state Kansas to the hundreds of Missourians who rode all night to burn the town at dawn. Bushwhackers under the control of William Quantrill murdered every man and boy they could find, killing well over one hundred. Four days later the U.S. Army, in what could be seen as either a wise precaution or a vicious act of revenge, declared part of Missouri completely evacuated. Military Order No. 11 directed that everyone living in a four-county area along the Kansas border "remove from their present places of residence within fifteen days." Unionist Missourians were permitted to move to designated military outposts or to Kansas; those who did not have certificates of loyalty had to leave. The roads south of Kansas City were filled with frightened and angry refugees in carts, on horseback, and on foot, carrying their belongings tied up in their quilts and bedding.

In 1929 Ruby Short McKim, a quilt pattern designer from Independence, Missouri, retold the story in her newspaper column in the *Kansas City Star*. "Fannie Kreeger Haller, a 10-year-old girl, saw her mother's choice new quilt snatched from their bed by maurauders back in 18— when Order No. 11 was the issue. She carried the treasured design in her mind and years after reproduced the quilt, christening it "Order No. 11."[95]

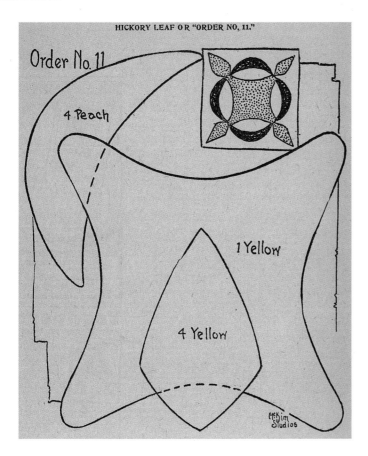

Order No. 11 pattern as it appeared in the Kansas City Star in 1929.

Quilt historian Florence Peto also used the name Order No. 11 to describe the pattern in her 1939 book, *Historic Quilts*. "Somewhere near Chattanooga during Reconstruction days following the War Between the States, a quilt was resurrected. It had been buried in the ground with other treasures by a fleeing housewife when news of advancing Union soldiers spread terror through her village. When the quilt came to light its pattern exulted admiration and puzzlement for it was one not familiar to Southern quiltmakers. It was copied and named after the Military Order for Evacuation, Order Number 11."[96]

Peto has moved the story to east Tennessee, buried the quilt, and made it an unfamiliar design. Her story seems to be a derivation of McKim's newspaper folklore, showing how tales printed by the commercial quilt pattern network can re-enter the oral tradition.

The pattern that Fannie remembered is an old one, one of the appliqué designs that became popular in the 1830s and 1840s. It has many other names, among them Hickory Leaf, the Orange Peel, and the Reel. McKim showed it as two colors with nine pieces. This easy version by Terry Clothier Thompson is cut paper-snowflake-fashion from a single piece of fabric. The stars in the sashing add a patriotic air to a quilt that recalls an important event in the War.

Size: 56½" x 56½"
Blocks: 12" finished

FABRIC REQUIREMENTS

- Blocks: 9 fat quarters of various blue prints
- Stars and background of the blocks: 1¾ yards yellow
- Sashing: 1 yard blue print
- Sashing: ¾ yard of red print
- Background of the stars: ⅝ yard of a different red print
- Backing: 3½ yards
- Binding: ½ yard (See Binding page 123.)

CUTTING AND SEWING

Order No. 11 Blocks

Cut nine 13" squares from the yellow background fabric. The squares are cut a little larger and then trimmed to 12½" after the appliqué is finished, because the appliqué can sometimes draw up the background. Make a template for the blue appliqué shapes. From each fat quarter, cut a 13" square. Fold corner to corner, and then in half again, with the right side of the fabric out. Place the template along the folds as directed. Draw around the template with a pencil or a fine-line permanent marker. Pin through the four layers and cut out the shape, adding the seam allowance as you cut. Mark the center with a pin.

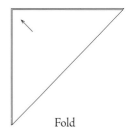

Fold

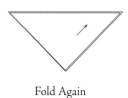

Fold Again

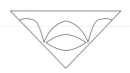

Place template along folds.

Adjust the seam allowance according to the way you will be appliquéing. Fold your background squares in half, and then in half again, to find the center. Pin and baste the appliqué to the background blocks, making sure the shape is centered and ½" away from the edges. Press to remove the folds if needed. Appliqué by hand or machine. Terry did most of the blocks using a top stitch on the machine with blue thread in both the bobbin and needle. She sewed an ⅛" from the basted edge of the appliqué. We've found many Civil War era quilts appliquéd in this fashion. Trim the blocks to 12½". If you've machine appliquéd the shapes you can press again. Terry never presses hand appliquéd edges.

Star Blocks

There are 16 yellow stars with a red background. Templates are given for appliqué or piecing; choose the one best for you. If you are appliquéing, cut sixteen 6" squares of red. Cut the stars from the yellow fabric and appliqué. Trim to 5½" square. If you have decided to piece, make templates. Terry makes them without seam allowances, then traces on the back of the fabric with a pencil so she has a line to stitch on. Add ¼" seam allowance as you cut. Stitch only on the lines; you will be stopping ¼" from the edges to set-in the background pieces with Y seams. Follow the stitching order carefully. Stitch pieces B to A to B together. Then stitch pieces C to C together. Stitch these two units together to create the star. Set in the background starting with D, then E. Set in piece Dr and Er. Last is piece F. Note: Be careful not to stretch pieces when stitching since there are many bias edges being stitched together.

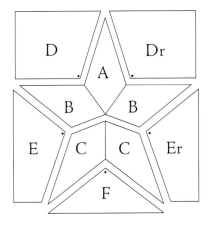

Star Piecing Order

Sashing

The sashing is a unit consisting of two blue 2" strips and one red 3" strip. Cut 16 strips of blue 2" wide selvage to selvage. Cut 8 strips of red 3" wide selvage to selvage. Stitch the strips together with the red in the middle and blue on either side. Press. Cut twenty-four 12" x ½" units from these strips for the sashing.

Stitching the Top Together

Following the illustration, stitch four stars with three sashing strips. You'll need four. Stitch three Order No. 11 blocks with four sashing strips in between and on the ends. You'll need three. Stitch the rows together to complete the top.

Quilting

See Utility Quilting on page 122. If you used a solid background for your appliqué you might want to do a fancier type of quilting; for example, echo quilt around the shape of the appliqué and put rows of stars in the sashing.

For tips on batting and binding see General Instructions beginning on page 122.

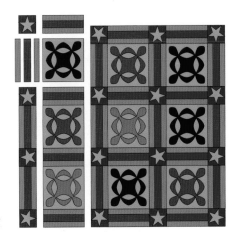

Quilt Top Construction

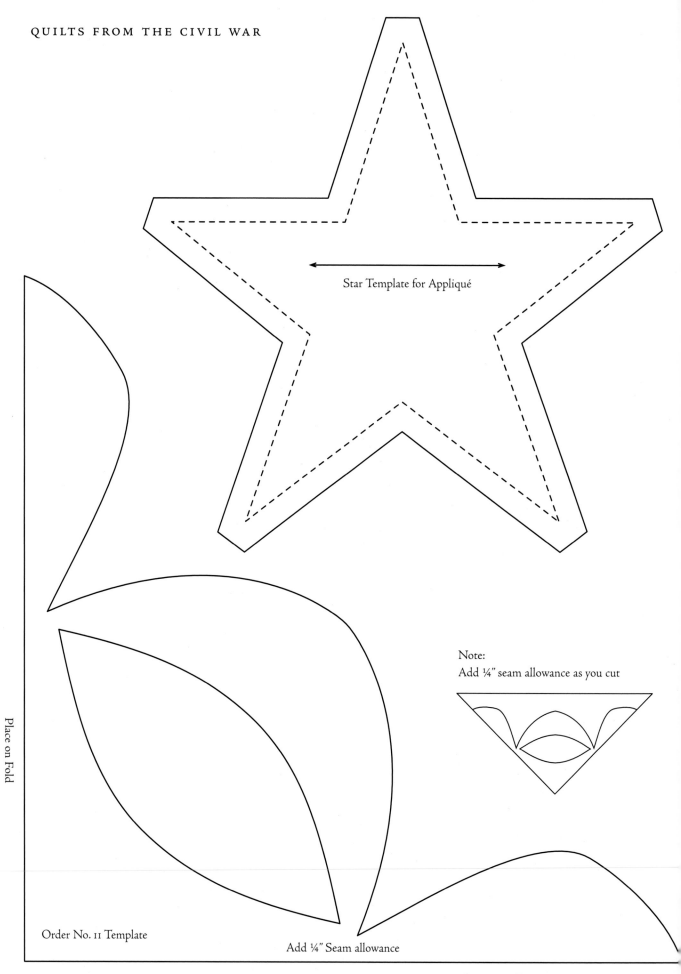

Star Template for Appliqué

Note:
Add ¼" seam allowance as you cut

Place on Fold

Order No. 11 Template

Add ¼" Seam allowance

Place on Fold

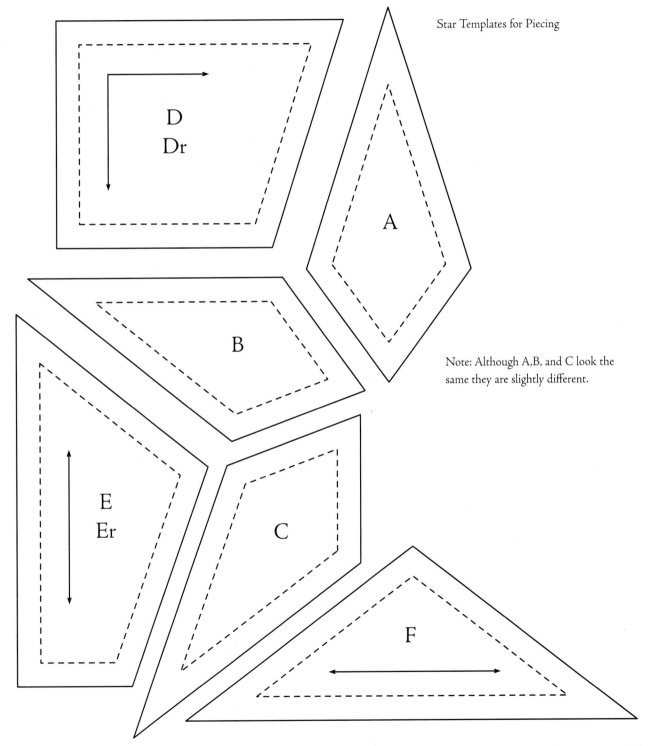

Star Templates for Piecing

D
Dr

A

B

Note: Although A,B, and C look the same they are slightly different.

E
Er

C

F

Pea Ridge Lily

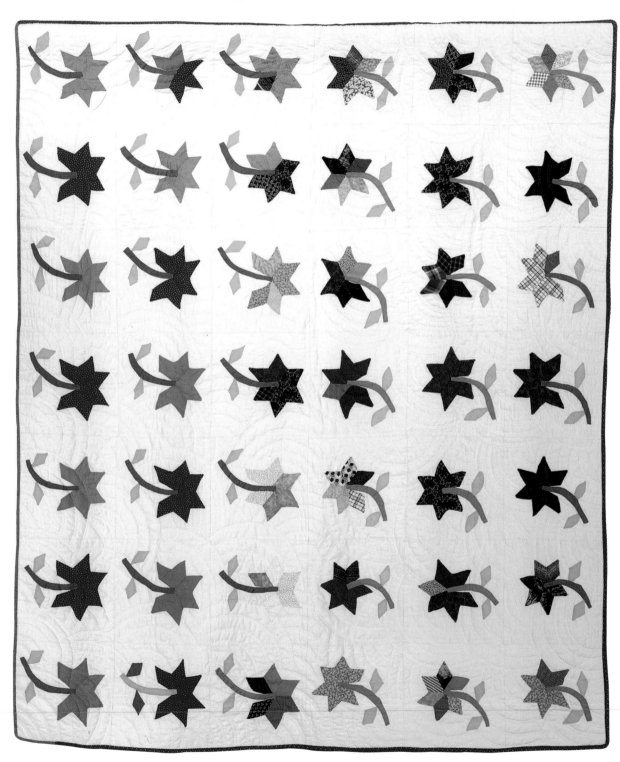

Pea Ridge Lily by Jeananne Wright,
Longmont, Colorado, 1996

The original of this quilt (page 94) is said to have been buried to keep it safe while Union soldiers ransacked northern Arkansas. In a cold March in 1862, Federal troops occupying Missouri marched south to confront rebel soldiers determined to regain Missouri for the Confederacy. Over 10,000 Union soldiers chased retreating Confederates into the Ozarks. Supplies were scarce and the soldiers on both sides were encouraged to forage for food, animal feed, and other day-to-day necessities. The two-day battle, a Union victory, was one of the most significant engagements in the West. Nearly 2500 men died and Missouri remained a Union state.

Military historians William L. Shea and Earl J. Hess, in their book *Pea Ridge: Civil War Campaign in the West*, note that "Pea Ridge was an enormous event in the lives of its participants," one that generated "a wealth of folk memories expressed in song and story." Tales of quilts being buried are part of that wealth of folk memory. The stains on the original might have been caused by any disaster, large or small—from a leaky roof, to a flood, to a battle. The spots, which might easily be cleaned, have become part of the quilt's history and its myth. We have little evidence of this quilt's connection to the Battle of Pea Ridge, other than a note pinned to it. The quilt is old enough to have survived the battle; the prints in the lilies could easily date from the 1850s. The stems were once all green but some have faded to brown.[97]

Jeananne Wright has reproduced the *Pea Ridge Lily* from her collection of antique quilts. The design, a version of the classic eight-pointed star, has many names. The oldest in print is Sweet Gum Leaf from Clara Stone's pattern designs about 1910. But the design is more likely a Lily, a name Carlie Sexton gave it in the 1920s.

The block can be done in a combination of piecing and appliqué, but the original is all appliqué. In the original some of the lilies contain six diamonds of identical fabric. In others the maker (Mrs. Pope?) has mixed the materials in a rather random way, which is part of the charm of this quilt. Jeananne made a faithful copy, looking for reproduction prints to match each of the blocks.

Size: 66½" x 77½"
Blocks: 11" finished

FABRIC REQUIREMENTS

- Background: 5 yards of ecru, tan, or off-white cotton. I advise against using unbleached muslin for reproductions. Mid-nineteenth century women did not use it in their quilts. It is an inexpensive weave of inexpensive yarns full of slubs and other brown specks. The low thread count and coarse yarns may look nostalgically old-fashioned, but the fabric shrinks and wrinkles. If you want that unbleached color you are better off with a good 100% cotton broadcloth of an off-white or yellowish tan. Avoid bright, bluish whites since cotton yellows with age, and it is that slightly yellowed look that we admire in old quilts.

- Flowers: The flowers are made of scrap-bag cottons. Flannels appear in the original, along with plaids, stripes, checks, and small florals. You will need a total of 1½ yards of scraps; or buy fat quarters in a range of warm browns, soft pinks, bright and navy blues, and Turkey reds for the lilies.
- Leaves: ⅓ yard of plain bright yellow-orange solid. The two leaves on each stem are what nineteenth-century dyers called chrome orange; what we might call safety yellow or cheddar.
- Stems: The stems are both green and tan; You'll need ⅓ yard total.
- Backing: 4 yards
- Binding: ½ yard (See Binding page 123.)

CUTTING AND SEWING

Background

Cut forty-two 11½" squares from the background fabric.

Lilies

The maker used a top stitch for hand appliqué. We were surprised at how many Civil War era quilts we saw that were top stitched by hand using a running stitch, as this one was. After trying the technique we were pleased to find it was simple and very fast. Prepare your appliqué pieces by basting or pressing the edges under, then arrange the pieces on the background. Thread a needle with a single thread and stitch through the appliqué and background with a running stitch close to the edge, being sure to go through all the layers. Knots go on the back with thread tails trimmed.

In some blocks Jeananne has saved time by cutting double diamonds and has appliquéd three of them to make a flower. Use the template as a single diamond or double diamond. Mix them in whichever way pleases you.

Leaves

There are 84 leaves. In the quilt some of the diamond shaped leaves round out, so two templates are given, one for diamond-shaped leaves and one for oval leaves. Mix these as well.

Stems

The 42 stems are green and/or tan. The stems are cut from strips of bias 1¼" x 7" long. Carefully fold and press both raw edges ¼". Position leaves under the stem and appliqué as desired.

Setting

This quilt has a classic nineteenth-century set, with half the blocks going east and the other half going west. We have a tendency today to think of our quilts as wallhangings with a definite up and down directionality. Yet many nineteenth-century patterns are set so the quilts can be viewed from any direction. This is a quilt that was meant to be seen on a bed. Set your finished blocks in six rows of seven blocks, block to block. Be sure three rows face one direction; three rows another. There is no sashing or border on this simple Southern quilt.

Quilting

The original is quilted in the fans design (see General Instructions, page 122.) Like so many quilters of the Civil War era, Mrs. Pope quilted right over her appliquéd design.

For tips on binding and batting see General Instructions, page 122. Bind with a color from one of the flowers.

Quilt Top Construction

Tips for Reproduction Fabrics

Although green is the color of nature, dyers found it impossible to obtain a colorfast green dye from natural plants and minerals. To get a viable green they had to dye cotton first blue, then yellow (or vice versa). This worked quite well if both blue and yellow were equally colorfast, but the blues they used (Prussian blue) were not particularly washfast. Prussian blue had a tendency to fade to tan in alkalai solutions such as soap or detergent. When the blue began to fade the greens took on a distinct yellowish cast, because the yellow usually stood up to washing. When looking for mid-nineteenth-century reproduction greens keep your eyes open for yellowish-green tints. Do avoid the sea-foam, misty greens we love so much today. You want something greener and harsher for an authentic nineteenth-century look.

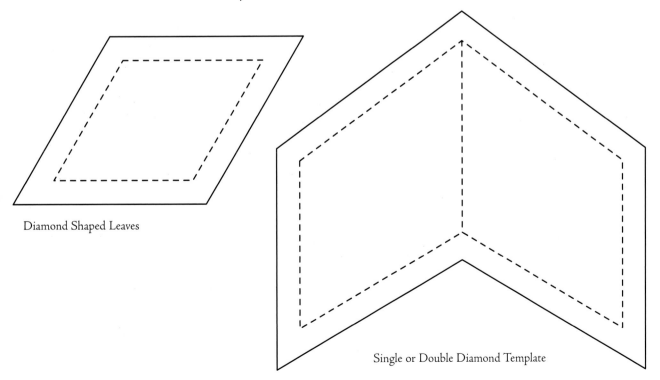

Diamond Shaped Leaves

Single or Double Diamond Template

Pea Ridge Lily Block

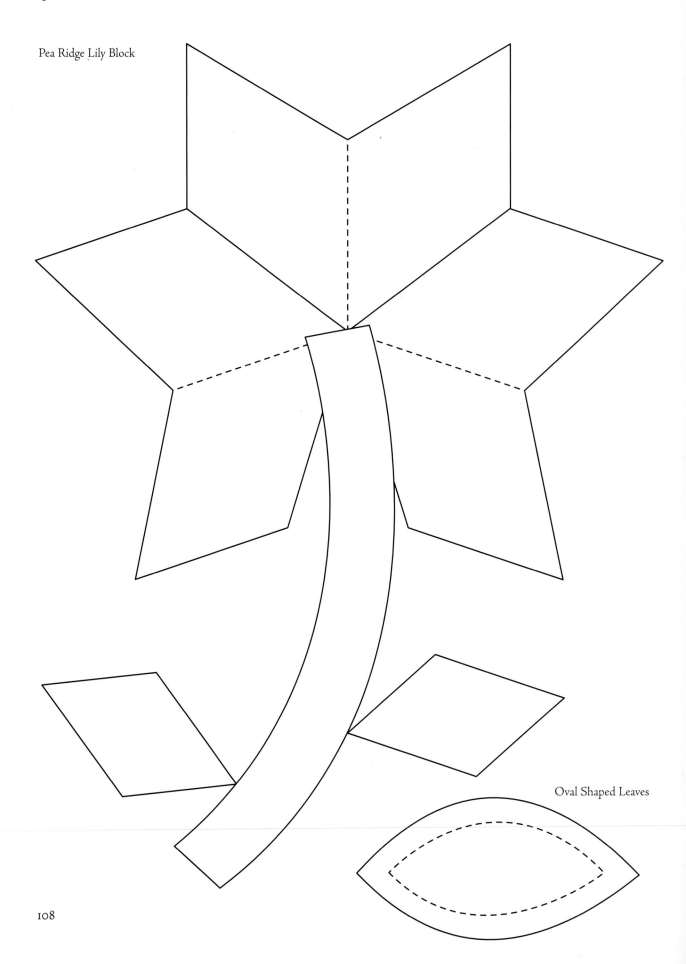

Oval Shaped Leaves

CHAPTER 8

"Every Star Brighter than Before," Commemorative Quilts

May 1, 1865. "So the 'rebellion is over! Four long years of the most terrible and bloody warfare any nation every endured, and the old flag floats triumphant over us again—with its glory undimmed and every star brighter than before."

May 2, 1865. "The official announcement of the death of the President only reached us to-day. . . . The colored people are frightened and apprehensive. They feel a personal loss, and fear the result of it to themselves." [98]

Diary of Esther Hill Hawkes

Esther Hill Hawkes's diary entries only a day apart contrast her joy and grief. Her words illuminate the ultimate tragedy of the Civil War. Celebration of Union victory at Appomatox Courthouse on April 9th, 1865, was immediately turned upside down by Lincoln's assassination a week later. Across the North women wrote of their shock and sorrow. After hearing the newsboys call out the headlines, Charlotte Woolsey wrote her sister Eliza, "What can one do? We are dumb with grief. The extra has just been cried giving the awful moment of his death. What a moment for America!" Maggie Lindsley addressed her diary, "Even here in this small Indiana town, so far from the scene of the appalling tragedy, the horror and sorrow are intense. Tears are in all eyes—sobs in every voice—old men and children, rich and poor, white and black—all feel it a personal loss." [99]

To Southern eyes like Sarah Morgan's the tidings of Lee's surrender were "dreadful. Every body cried, but I would not, satisfied that God will still save us, even though all should apparently be lost." Stories abound of Southerners arrested for rejoicing at Lincoln's death, but Sarah viewed Lincoln's assassin John Wilkes Booth as a murderer. "Let historians extol blood shedding; it is woman's place to abhor it." [100]

Lincoln's funeral was held in Springfield, Illinois, his last hometown. As the train carrying his remains wended across the Union, towns and cities draped themselves in mourning to receive the body of the slain hero. The Indiana Quilt Project found a Log Cabin quilt made, the story goes, from the black crepe that wrapped the columns of the Indianapolis State House. William Robert Latta bought some of

Homage to Elizabeth by Bobbi Finley,
San Jose, California, 1996

Bobbi Finley stitched a faithful copy of a
patriotic quilt, probably made to celebrate
Grant's 1869 inauguration. The words
remember the martyred president
Abraham Lincoln and Grant Pr(esident)
and Colfax Vi(ce-president). The words
Union Star in the lower right tell us how
important star imagery was to the Union
cause. The original was "made by
Elizabeth Holmes in her 68th year."

the fabric after the funeral to give to his wife Rebecca and daughters
Alice and Mary, who made a design in the Barn-Raising set.[101]

Log Cabin quilts became quite popular in the years after the War.
Many may have been made as mourning quilts, a symbolism that we no
longer read. But most were probably the result of a fad that made them
so common that agricultural fairs had prize categories exclusively for
Log Cabins in the last decades of the century. Some Log Cabin quilts
are passed down with the story that they were made from the uniforms
of returning soldiers, but I have never personally found one that
can be documented to be of Northern uniform fabric (it would seem
unlikely any Confederate sympathizer would make a Log Cabin quilt
to remember the Lost Cause).

Uniform fabric is said to be the source of many other types of wool quilts. For example, The West Virginia Historical Quilt Survey found a wool comforter made by Louisa Thomas Bunten in 1875 from her husband Lieutenant Watson Morgan Bunten's uniform. As with other quilts tied to the War, its story, which may indeed be true, is hard to prove. There was so much variety in uniforms, especially in the South, that many quilts of various wools are assigned the same origins.[102]

Several memorial quilts leave no question as to the maker's intent, as words and portraits give us a code that is easy to read. The Chicago Historical Society's Nunda Lodge quilt, made in McHenry, Illinois, features the words "It's Old Abe Forever" in the center. The Birmingham Museum of Art has displayed a crazy quilt made by Martha Douglas Montgomery of Montgomery, Alabama. Active in the Ladies Confederate Memorial Association, Martha covered her silk quilt with watercolor portraits of Generals from both North and South and included a large white star cut from the flag that flew above the inauguration of Jefferson Davis as President of the Confederate States of America. Robert E. Lee's wife Mary Custis Lee made a medallion quilt to raise funds for a memorial chapel. Mrs. Lee's quilt is in the collection of the Virginia Military Institute. Pocahontas Virginia Gay made two picture quilts of wools and silks in the early twentieth century. The one in the Smithsonian Institution's collection features painted portraits of Jefferson Davis and Generals Robert E. Lee and Stonewall Jackson among appliquéd dog and horse blocks.[103]

The cover of *Needlecraft* magazine occasionally pictured period quilters. In this issue, published in December, 1929, a Civil War quilter is putting the finishing touches on a Log Cabin quilt in the Courthouse Steps set.

Confederate Commemorative Quilt by Varina Davis, about 1870. Silk. Collection of the Museum of the Confederacy, Richmond, Virginia. Photograph courtesy of the Museum.

There is no doubt about First Lady Varina Davis's intentions in this silk quilt commemorating the Confederate States of America. Three Confederate flags and a Confederate shield fill the corners. When her granddaughter Varina Davis Hayes Webb donated the quilt to the Museum of the Confederacy she included notes explaining the symbolism in the embroidery. Oak leaves mean "The long-lived evergreen–growth and dignity of the Confederacy." Ivy–"the faithful loyal binding together of a warrior people." The passion flower and the bleeding heart in the lower left recall "the suffering heroines of the southern cause and people." The olive branch surrounding the butterfly symbolizes "the peace of the future to a cause that lost but held its victors crown of peace." And the butterfly–"the soul of the Confederacy beautiful and immortal." We can hope that making this quilt to honor the Lost Cause gave her some solace as we remember her despairing words to Mary Chesnut in 1864, "I cannot read—but I sew *hard*."

Quilts remained an important part of
American life after the War. These Texas
families pose before the simple warm
coverings typically made by Southern
rural women.

A membership badge in the Grand
Army of the Republic, the major Civil
War veteran's association.

The Women's Relief Corps, the ladies'
auxiliary of the G.A.R., adopted a Maltese
cross as their symbol. The image is found
on end-of-the-century signature quilts,
a clue to a relationship to the veteran's
organization.

The largest post-War organization for women was the Women's Relief Corps of the Grand Army of the Republic, the Union Army veteran's association. Founded in the year after the war, the G.A.R. continued active until the last veteran died in 1956.

Many women must have crafted quilts to honor the G.A.R. and raise funds for its causes. Magazines at the turn of the century published quilt patterns with suggestions like this: "Susanna's Puzzle is very effective when made with red, white and blue and in this way is just the thing for a G.A.R. or W.R.C. fair." "The Double Star makes a beautiful quilt for a G.A.R. or W.R.C. Fair. Make the outside of red, the back star of blue and the center one white. If the date 1861 is worked on the white everyone will recognize the significance. M.E.B." [104]

Tree of Paradise by Barbara Brackman, Lawrence, Kansas, 1983-1996. Quilted by Didi Salvatierri. Collection of Pamela Rugen.

I made this copy of an antique quilt for my niece, using reproduction navy blue prints and the reds that are just a little too orange to be faithful copies of the nineteenth-century Turkey reds. I saw the original at a quilt show years ago; it looked to be from about 1890-1920. Now I wonder how many of these red, white, and blue quilts, so typical of the turn-of-the-century era, were made as G.A.R. commemoratives and fund-raisers.

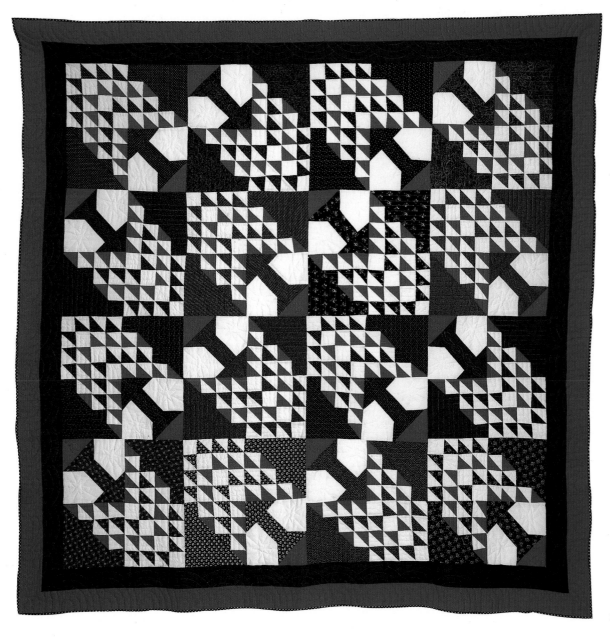

Veteran's Flag by Gail Bakkom,
Minneapolis, Minnesota, 1996, 87″ x 72″

The inspiration for Gail's quilt, made by
Emma Van Fleet in 1866, is in the collection of the Yakima Valley Museum in
Yakima, Washington. Gail's faithful copy
honors Joseph W. Britton whose life
became intertwined with her husband's
family although they never met. In 1882
eighteen-year-old Hans Hanse was haul-
ing freight for the government at Fort
Sisseton, South Dakota. On the parade
ground he found a tiny silver shield
inscribed with the name Joseph W. Britton.
Too young to recall the Civil War, Hanse
kept the souvenir and passed it down to
his grandson, Jim Bakkom, who treasures
it. Jim traced Britton through pension
records, discovering that he was a New
Yorker who enlisted in Company E of
the 3rd Minnesota Infantry and fought
in numerous battles. Jim's wife Gail made
this quilt as a gift for him, recording
Britton's Civil War service. She included
a reproduction of the silver badge.

Emma Van Fleet's original version of
the flag pattern was made to commemo-
rate Sergeant Alfred A. Van Fleet's forty-
six battles in 1862 and 1863. Van Fleet was
with Company K of the 18th Illinois State
Cavalry.

The irony is of course that today we would not recognize the
significance. A red, white, and blue quilt with the date 1861 easily might
be interpreted as a quilt made during the war. These newspaper
clippings are tantalizing clues to the meaning of some turn-of-the-
last-century quilts. Certainly red, white, and blue was a popular color
scheme in the 1890-1925 era. We have difficulty interpeting the
symbolism—if any symbolism was intended. Were the quilts in the
colors of the flag made for a G.A.R. fair, a Spanish-American War victory celebration, or to reflect World War I patriotism? Or was red, white,
and blue just a good combination of colors?

As with so many other questions about quilts connected to the
Civil War, we must interpret the quilts using evidence in the fabrics, the
patterns, and the stories that are handed down with them. We also must
be aware of the historical and social context in which they were made.
Certainly quilts give us much insight into that context. As one of the
few objects left from the era, they keep us connected to the women of
the past, the women who lived through the War.

Log Fence

Log Fence, made by a member of the
Burkhart Family, possibly in west-central,
Illinois, 1860-1875, Collection of Barbara
and Kern Jackson

Little is known about the origins of this quilt from Barbara Jackson's family, but the wool fabrics are the delaines so important for clothing during the War era. It may have been a desire to make quilts of the popular delaines, challis, and barége (combination fabrics that could be fairly sheer) that inspired quiltmakers to begin piecing on foundations. The technique is definitely from the 1860s. It's nice to imagine that it is a Civil War era quilt, possibly inspired by the Log Cabin image linked to the martyred president.

The design is a simplified version of the Log Cabin, one I have never seen before, more like the Fence Rail pattern, which doesn't have a square in the center. Since it's a combination of both designs I've called it Log Fence, a reference to Abraham Lincoln, known for splitting logs to build rail fences.

Mrs. Burkhart used both reds and blacks as the centers for her blocks. She pieced the wool strips to a cotton foundation, but the instructions here are for using a paper foundation method.

The original is scraps of light-weight wool and cotton blend fabrics, a material that is difficult to find today. You may want to use the pattern for a sampler of your Civil War reproduction calicoes. This quilt would also be a good way to show off the taffetas, satins, and brocades that re-enactors are wearing in their ball gowns today. Of course, silk is preferable to synthetics, but only a few re-enactors are using real silk. Silk and its synthetic imitations are hard to piece using conventional piecing (they slip around too much), so this pattern with its paper support is good for a sampler of ball dress fabrics.

If you are going to a ball, pack self-addressed, stamped envelopes, and ask the best-dressed ladies to mail you strips of their fabric 2″ by 7″ (the extra gives you room to trim to the right size).

Size: 30½″ x 36½″
Blocks: 6″ finished

FABRIC REQUIREMENTS

- Blocks: 210 different fabrics or a total of 1½ yards of fabric. You'll probably want to repeat some of the fabrics as Mrs. Burkhart did.
- Backing: 1 yard
- Binding: ⅜ yard (See Binding on page 123.)

CUTTING AND SEWING

Cutting the Block Strips

For the centers cut thirty 1½″ squares. The original quilt has both red and black centers. Cut strips 1½″ x 6½″ until you have a total of 210 strips. You'll be cutting one long strip into two short ones for the center, but do that cutting while you are piecing. Since you are going to paper piece the design on the machine, your cutting needn't be so precise—

one of the great advantages of the new paper piecing method.

Paper Piecing the Blocks

Photocopy thirty blocks of the Log Fence pattern (page 118). Be careful, some photocopy machines distort the copy in one direction. (If you are one of those paper piecers who loves to work small, you can reduce the size of the block.)

For each block, turn the paper pattern over so the fabric goes on the blank side. Begin with a 1½″ square of fabric, or something a little larger. Pin the square to the center of the paper, lining it up by holding the pattern up to the light. Choose a fabric for the center strip and cut it in half. Pin a short strip to one side, right sides together. Be sure the strip fits correctly in the pattern lines by holding it up to the light and pinning to the paper. With the printed pattern facing up, machine stitch the strip down on the short horizontal line. Finger press it open. Repeat for the other side using the leftover fabric to finish the strip. Add the other six strips in the order shown on the pattern, pinning and holding the paper up to the light as you go. Trim now if the overhang gets in your way, but it's most efficient to trim at the end. After each seam, finger press the "log" as you hide the seam. Trim the finished block to 6½″ square, which includes the ¼″ seam allowance marked on the paper pattern. If you are using cotton for your logs you may remove the paper backing at this point and stitch the blocks together. If you are using silks or synthetics, stitch the blocks into the top before tearing off the paper for a more accurate set. Stitch the blocks as shown in the diagram, alternating horizontal and vertical directionality.

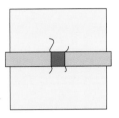

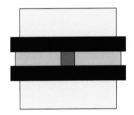

Paper Piecing

Quilting

Quilting silk is often quite frustrating, as the lines never have that crisp look of cotton, so you might want to tack this quilt with small knots (on the back) in the corners of each block. Mrs. Burkhart just bound the quilt with a knitted wool braid, leaving her fabric foundations showing on the back, a typical thing to do at that time when neat backs weren't as important in needlework as they are today. If you'd like to quilt your *Log Fence* you'll probably want to quilt in squares around the logs, or try the elbow quilting shown on page 122.

For tips on batting and binding see General Instructions beginning on page 122.

Log Fence Block; photocopy thirty blocks for paper piecing.

ENDNOTES

1 This quote is signed "M.W.C." in the January 12, 1838 edition of *Liberator*, 6.

2 *Liberator*, January 12, 1838, 6.

3 A. R. P. Danvers, *Liberator*, February 16, 1838, 8.

4 The quilt was described in the *Liberator* on January 2, 1837. A photographic detail of it has been published numerous times. I am grateful to historians Cuesta Benberry and Sandi Fox for calling our attention to an amazing document of women's role in the abolitionist movement, and to Merikay Waldvogel who measured the original and described it to me. For a photograph see Pat Ferrero, Elaine Hedges and Julie Silber, *Hearts and Hands: The Influence of Women & Quilts on American Society* (Nashville: Rutledge Hill Press, 1996), 72. The Rutledge Hill publication is a reprint of the 1987 edition from The Quilt Digest Press.

5 I am grateful to Ricki Maietta for informing me about the quilt at the Lycoming County Historical Society. The Chester County quilt is pictured in Pepper Cory and Susan McKelvey *The Signature Quilt: Traditions, Techniques & the Signature Block Collection.* (Saddle Brook, N.J., Quilt House, 1995).

6 The story about the Log Cabin quilts appears to have been published first in Gladys-Marie Fry, *Stitched From the Soul: Slave Quilts in the Ante-Bellum South* (New York: Dutton Studio Books, 1990), 52. She writes, "Log Cabin Quilts containing black fabric often served as signals on the Underground Railroad to identify 'safe houses.'" Raymond G. Dobard, "A Covenant in Cloth: The Visible and Tangible in African-American Quilts," in Janice Tauer Wass (ed.), *Connecting Stitches: Quilts in Illinois Life* (Springfield: Illinois State Museum, 1995), 33.

7 Diary entry by Rachel Bowman Cormany, James C. Mohr (ed.), *The Cormany Diaries: A Northern Family in the Civil War* (Pittsburgh: University of Pittsburgh Press, 1982), 94, 104-105.

8 Levi Coffin, "*Reminiscences*" (Cincinnati,

1875), 304-11. Quoted in *American History As Told By Contemporaries* (New York: MacMillan, 1901), 83.

9 Mrs. C. I. H. Nichols, *Wyandotte Gazette*, December 29, 1882.

10 Barbara Brackman, *Clues in the Calico: A Guide to Identifying and Dating Antique Quilts* (McLean, Virginia: EPM Publications, 1989), 144, 170-1. Virginia Gunn, "Quilts For Union Soldiers In the Civil War," Sally Garoutte (ed.) *Uncoverings 1985 Vol. 6* (Mill Valley, California: American Quilt Study Group, 1986), 108.

11 Ruth Finley, *Old Patchwork Quilts and the Women Who Made Them* (Philadelphia: J. B. Lippincott, 1929), reprint (McLean, Virginia: EPM Publications, 1992), 70-1.

12 William Still, *The Underground Railroad* (Philadelphia: Porter and Coates, 1872), reprint (New York: Arno Press, 1968), 212. Harriet Beecher Stowe, *Uncle Tom's Cabin* (Boston: John P. Jewett, 1852), reprint (New York: Harper & Row, 1965), 52.

13 W. D. McKinistry, *Selections of Editorial Miscellanies and Letters*, (Fredonia, New York: By the Author, 1894).

14 Letter from Eliza Horton to Emma Barbour, August 2, 1860. Shirley Blotnik Moskow (ed.), *Emma's World: An Intimate Look at Lives Touched by the Civil War Era* (Far Hills, New Jersey: New Horizon Press, 1990), 44. Letter from Sarah Watkins to her daughter, Letitia Watkins Walton, November 2, 1860. E. Grey Dimond and Herman Hattaway, *Letters from Forest Place: A Plantation Family's Correspondence, 1846-1881* (Jackson: University Press of Mississippi, 1993), 187.

15 Robert E. Denney, *The Civil War Years: A Day-by-Day Chronicle of the Life of a Nation* (New York: Sterling Publishing, 1992), 27. Diary entry by Ada W. Bacot, January 24, 1861. Jean V. Berlin (ed.) *A Confederate Nurse: The Diary of Ada W. Bacot* (Columbia, University of South Carolina Press, 1994), 26.

16 "An Englishman in South Carolina," *Continental Monthly* 2 (1862), 689-94 and

3 (1863), 110-117. Quoted in *American History as Told by Contemporaries* #568.

17 *Peterson's Magazine*, June, 1861. Elizabeth Moffitt Lyle's quilt, in the collection of the Smoky Hill Museum, is pictured in Barbara Brackman and Jennie Chinn (eds.), *Kansas Quilts and Quilters* (Lawrence: University Press of Kansas, 1993), 10. The album quilt belongs to Linda Critchfield, Van Nuys, California.

18 Jacqueline Marx Atkins, *Shared Threads: Quilting Together—Past and Present* (New York: Viking Studio Books, 1994). Caroline Cowles Richards, *Village Life in America, 1852-1872* (London: T.F. Unwin, 1912), reprint (Williamstown, Massachusetts: Corner House Publishers, 1972), 131.

19 Richards, diary entry for May 1861, 131.

20 Atkins, 92-4.

21 Annie Darden's diary entry is quoted in Roberson, Ruth Haslip (ed.), *North Carolina Quilts* (Chapel Hill: University of North Carolina Press, 1988), 4. The Arkansas secession quilt is pictured in Arkansas Quilters Guild, *Arkansas Quilts* (Paducah, Kentucky: American Quilters Society), 20.

22 Myron Orlofsky and Patsy Orlofsky, *Quilts in America* (New York: McGraw Hill, 1974), reprint (New York: Abbeville Press, 1992), 206-9.

23 The letter to the newspaper is quoted in Bryding Adams Henley, "Alabama Gunboat Quilts," in Laurel Horton and Sally Garoutte (eds.), *Uncoverings 1987, Volume 8* (San Francisco: American Quilt Study Group, 1989), 13. The article has been reprinted as Bryding Adams, "Alabama Gunboat Quilts," in Laurel Horton (ed.), *Quiltmaking in America: Beyond the Myths* (Nashville: Rutledge Hill Press, 1994).

24 Lucy Larcom's words are quoted in Elizabeth Leonard, *Yankee Women: Gender Battles in the United States Civil War* (New York: W.W. Norton, 1994) 205. Diary entry by Sarah Morgan, May 17, 1862. Charles East (ed.), *The Civil War Diary of Sarah Morgan* (Athens: University of Georgia Press, 1991), 77.

Diary entry by Mary Chesnut, September 24, 1861. C. Vann Woodward (ed.), *Mary Chesnut's Civil War* (New Haven: Yale University Press, 1981), 199-200.

[25] H. T. Merrill, "Take Your Gun and Go, John." Willard A. and Porter W. Heaps, *The Singing Sixties: The Spirit of the Civil War Days Drawn From the Music of the Times* (Norman: University of Oklahoma Press, 1960), 95.

[26] *The 1856 Ward Bridal Quilt* (Charleston, South Carolina: Cobblestone Quilters Guild, 1992), 16.

[27] Richards, 114, 130-1.

[28] Diary entry by Emily Hawley Gillespie. Judy Nolte Lensink (ed.), *A Secret To Be Buried: The Diary and Life of Emily Hawley Gillespie* (Iowa City: University of Iowa Press, 1989), 66. Memoirs of Sarah Jane Full Hill. Mark M. Krug (ed.), *Mrs. Hill's Journal: Civil War Reminiscences* (Chicago: R. R. Donnelley and Sons, 1980), 48-9.

[29] Letter to her father from Charlotte Wilson. Nancy Coffey Heffernan and Ann Page Stecker, *Sisters of Fortune* (Hanover: University Press of New England, 1993), 261. Charlotte mentions lint, as do many other chroniclers of the War. During the first years of treating battle wounds doctors believed that packing a wound with lint scraped from cotton or linen was an effective treatment method. Men went into battle prepared with bundles of lint scraped by sisters and wives. They soon discovered that lint only added to the infection, and discussions of scraping lint no longer appeared in diaries and letters.

[30] Letter from Abby Woolsey to her sister Eliza, May 17, 1861. Geogeanna Woolsey Bacon and Eliza Woolsey Howland *Letters of A Family During the War for the Union* (New York: Privately Printed 1899), 76.

[31] United States Sanitary Commission, *Report Concerning the Woman's Central Association of Relief at New York*. October 12, 1861, 24.

[32] Virginia Gunn, "Quilts for Union Soldiers in the Civil War," Laurel Horton (ed.), *Quiltmaking in America:*

Beyond the Myths (Nashville: Rutledge Hill Press, 1994), 114.

[33] Quote from Southworth. Diary entries by Mary Chesnut, August 17, 1861, and May 23, 1862, Woodward 149, 344-5.

[34] Chesnut diary entry February 26, 1864, Woodward 573-4. Letter from Varina Davis to Mary Chesnut, October 8, 1864, entered in Chesnut's diary, 663.

[35] Diary entry for Nov. 26, 1862. Mary D. Robertson (ed), *Lucy Breckenridge of Grove Hill: The Diary of A Virginia Girl.* Kent, Kents, 1979, 75.

[36] Letter from William T. Sherman to David F. Boyd, December 24, 1860, quoted in Denney, 20.

[37] Diary entries by Catherine Edmonston for April 29, May 1, and July 8, 1861, Beth G. Crabtree and James W. Palten (Raleigh, North Carolina: Division of Archives & History, 1979) 57, 88.

[38] Chesnut diary entries for August 18 and September 2, 1861, 155-6, 195.

[39] James Welch Patton (ed.), *Minutes of the Proceedings of the Greenville Ladies' Assoiation in Aid of the Volunteers of the Confederate Army* (Durham: Duke University/ Trinity College Historical Society, 1937), 27, 65, 66, 70.

[40] Letter from Sarah Watkins to Leticia Watkins Walton, McGuire, February 24, 1862, 263.

[41] Edmonston diary entries for October 24 and 31 and November 13, 1862, 282-3, 287-8, 297.

[42] Patton, 86, 92.

[43] J. G. Forman, *The Western Sanitary Commission* (St. Louis: Mississippi Valley Sanitary Fair, 1864), 11.

[44] Letters to her mother from Cornelia Colton, December 28, 1863, and February 25, 1864. Betsey Gates (ed.), *The Colton Letters: Civil War Period 1861-1865* (Scottsdale: McLean Publications, 1993), 242, 268.

[45] Rex C. Myers (ed.), *Lizzie: Letters of Elizabeth Chester Fisk, 1864-1893* (1989), 7-11.

[46] See Jan Dodge's antique quilt in Gunn, 80.

[47] "An Englishman in South Carolina."

[48] Diary entries of Millie Gray, November 14 and 15, 1833. Fletcher Young (ed.),

Diary of Millie Gray, 1832-1840 (Galveston: Rosenher Library Press, 1967), 32.

[49] Letter from Rebecca Gratz to her sister-in-law, summer, 1834. David Philipson (ed.) *Letters of Rebecca Gratz* (Philadelphia: The Jewish Publication Society of America 1929), 199. Letter from Sherman. Anne L. Macdonald, *No Idle Hands: The Social History of American Knitting.* (New York: Ballantine Books, 1991) 112.

[50] Bacot, 49.

[51] Diary entries by Chesnut, April 2, 14 and 15, 1862. Woodward, 317, 324.

[52] Bryding Adams, 13.

[53] Diary entry by Mary Chesnut, June 2, 1862. Woodward, 354.

[54] Letter from Abby Woolsey to her sisters, March, 1862. Bacon and Howland, 264.

[55] Letter quoted in Agatha Young, *The Women and the Crisis: Women of the North in the Civil War* (New York: McDowell, Oblensky: 1959), 311.

[56] *Daily Alta California*, August 19, 1864, quoted in Dorothy H. Huggins, "Women in War-Time, San Francisco, The Ladies' Christian Commision Fair," *California Historical Society Quarterly*, Vol. 24, No. 2, June, 1945, 261-266.

[57] *Daily South Carolinian*, Columbia, January 4, 1865, 4. Dairy entries by Marny Chesnut, January 16-17, 1865. Woodward, 705.

[58] Lucy Larcom, "Call to Kansas," (to the air of Nelly Bly), a song in the *Liberator*, Vol. 25, #8, February 23, 1855, 32.

[59] Diary entry by Mary Chesnut, April 21, 1862. Woodward, 327.

[60] Diary entry by Sarah Morgan, no date but March, 1865. East, 597.

[61] Diary entry by Emma Holmes, August 15, 1864. 366.

[62] Richard Cleveland and Donna Bister, *Plain and Fancy: Vermont's People and Their Quilts as a Reflection of America* (Gualala, California: Quilt Digest Press 1991), 61. Brenda Manges Papadakis has copied the Stickle quilt and written a book about the experience, *Dear Jane: The Two Hundred Twenty-Five Patterns from the 1863 Jane Stickle Quilt* (Saddle Brook, New Jersey: Quilt House, 1996).

[63] Diary entry by Dolly Lunt Burge, 1862, quoted in Bets Ramsey, "The Quilter," *The Chattanooga Times*, August 14, 1986.

[64] Diary entry by Caroline Seabury, July 20, 1863. Suzanne L. Bunkers (ed.), *The Diary of Caroline Seabury, 1854-1863* (Madison: University of Wisconsin Press, 1991), 79.

[65] Rachel Maines discusses "Paradigms of Scarcity and Abundance/ The Quilt as an Artifact of the Industrial Revolution," in Jeannette Lasansky (ed.), *In the Heart of Pennsylvania: Symposium Papers* (Lewisburg, Pennsylvania: Oral Traditions Project, 1986).

[66] Diary entry by Cornelia McDonald, September, 1864. Gwin, pg. 210. Clay-Clopton, 223.

[67] Diary entry by Emma Holmes, October 8, 1864. Marszalek, 378. Diary entries by Mary Chesnut, March 5, 6, 1864, and March 18, 1865. Woodward, 588, 747-8.

[68] Letter from Lucy Chase, January 2, 1863. Henry L. Swint, *Dear Ones at Home: Letters from Contraband Camps* (Nashville: Vanderbilt University Press, 1966), 33.

[69] Diary entry by Catherine Edmonston, August 29, 1863. Patten, pg. 457. Clay-Clopton, 225.

[70] Diary entry by Sarah Morgan September 3, 1862. East, 234.

[71] The pattern is #1646 in Barbara Brackman, *Encyclopedia of Pieced Quilt Patterns*, (Paducah, Kentucky: American Quilters' Society, 1993)

[72] Mrs. Campbell Bryce, *The Personal Experiences of Mrs. Campbell Bryce During the Burning of Columbia, South Carolina* (Philadelphia: J. B. Lippincott, 1899), 16.

[73] Diary entry by Lucy Smith French, January 5, 1862. From the transcript of her diary in the Tennessee State Library and Archives. I am grateful to Bets Ramsey for this information.

[74] Letter from Mary Byson, March 21, 1864. Memoirs of Mrs. Mark Valentine, quoted in Katherine Jones, *Heroines of Dixie* (Indianapolis: Bobbs Merril: 1955) 275.

[75] Diary entry by Caroline Seabury, July 30, 1863. Bunkers, 91.

[76] Diary entry by Emma Holmes, January,

1864. Marszalek, 332.

[77] Letter to her mother from Tryphena Blanche Fox, Summer, 1864. King, 136-7, 139, 141.

[78] Diary entry by Emma Holmes, December 1, 1862. Marszalek, 215.

[79] Memories of September, 1864, by Cornelia Peake McDonald. Gwin, 204-5

[80] Merikay Waldvogel, "Southern Linsey Quilts of the Nineteenth Century," in Laurel Horton (ed.), *Quiltmaking in America: Beyond the Myths* (Nashville: Rutledge Hill Press, 1994). Bets Ramsey & Merikay Waldvogel, *Quilts of Tennessee* (Nashville: Rutledge Hill Press, 1986), 79.

[81] WPA interview with Lula Bowers, Luray, South Carolina. #W11051, June 28, 1938.

[82] E. Duane Elbert and Rachel Kamm Elbert, *History From the Heart: Quilt Paths Across Illinois* (Nashville: Rutledge Hill Press, 1993), 38-9.

[83] William Tecumseh Sherman, "March to the Sea 1864" in *American History as Told by Contemporaries*, 429.

[84] Diary entry by Mary Chesnut, February 25, 1865. Woodward, 733.

[85] Letter from Tryphena Blanche Fox to her mother. King, pg. 172. Letter from Sarah E. Watkins to her daughter, January 9, 1864. Dimond and Hattaway, pg. 314.

[86] Letter from Mary E. Robarts to her cousin, May 21, 1864. 1172. Diary entry by Ella Gertrude Thomas, September 3, 1864. Burr, 238. Robert Manson Myers (ed.) *Children of Pride: A True Story of Georgia and the Civil War.* (New Haven: Yale University Press, 1972)1172.

[87] Letter from Mary Jones Mallard to her mother, March 24, 1864. Myers, 1151.

[88] Testimony by Nancy Johnson, March 22, 1873. Ira Berlin, et al (eds.), *Free At Last* (New York: The New Press, 1992), 126-9.

[89] Sam Words's testimony in Paul D. Escott, *Slavery Remembered: A Record of Twentieth-Century Slave Narratives* (Chapel Hill: University of North Carolina Press, 1979), 124.

[90] Diary entry by Rachel Cormany, January 2, 1865. Mohr and Winslow, 500.

[91] Diary entry by Samuel Cormany, December 24 and 25, 1864. Mohr and Winslow, 507-8.

[92] Barbara Brackman, Mary Madden, Rebecca Martin, and Blair Tarr, *Material Pleasures: Quilts From the Kansas Museum of History* (Topeka: Kansas State Historical Society, 1995) 10.

[93] Ruth Haslip Roberson, 59.

[94] Diary entry by Sarah Morgan, September 3, 1862. East, 249.

[95] Ruby S. McKim, "Order Number 11," *Kansas City Star*, November 23, 1929.

[96] Florence Peto, *Historic Quilts* (New York: American Historical Co. 1949).

[97] William L. Shea and Earl J. Hess, *Pea Ridge: Civil War Campaign in the West* (Chapel Hill: University of North Carolina Press, 1992), 321.

[98] Diary entries by Esther Hill Hawkes, May 1, 2, 1865. Schwartz, 139.

[99] Letter from Charlotte Woolsey to her sister, April 15, 1865. Bacon and Howland, 659. Diary entry by Maggie Lindsley, April 15, 1865. Muriel Davies McKenzie (ed.), *Maggie Lindsley's Journal* (Nashville: Privately Printed, 1977), 83.

[100] Diary entry by Sarah Morgan, April 19, 1865. East, 606-7.

[101] Marilyn Goldman and Marguerite Wiebusch, *Quilts of Indiana: Crossroads of Memories* (Bloomington: Indiana University Press, 1991), 30-31.

[102] Letter to author from Fawn Valentine of the West Virginia Historical Quilt Survey, Quilt #3-0005, Upshur County.

[103] Varina Davis's and Mary Lee's quilts are described in Kimberly G. Sicola, *Stitched for a Cause: American Quilts of the Civil War Era, 1850-1870* (Richmond: Meadow Farm Museum, 1993). The Pocahontas Gay quilt in the Smithsonian collection is pictured in Doris M. Bowman *The Smithsonian Treasury: American Quilts* (Washington D.C.: Smithsonian Institution Press, 1991) 88.

[104] Undated clippings in a scrapbook owned by Merikay Waldvogel.

Utility Quilting

Elbow Quilting

APPENDICES

GENERAL INSTRUCTIONS

Batting

Cotton batting gives quilts an authentic, old-fashioned flat look, especially after a few washings. The problem with 100% cotton batting is that you will have to quilt it fairly closely, no more than 2″ between lines, because an all-cotton batt will shred in the wash if you don't quilt it enough. An alternative is the combination cotton/polyester battings that have just enough polyester in them to keep them together during washing. You can get away with less quilting and they still have a traditional look. Batting that is 100% polyester gives you a more modern look, but it is easier to needle and requires less quilting. If you are going to use 100% polyester, look for the low-loft type.

Utility Quilting

The best Civil War era quilts were quilted with some extraordinary quilting. It was the time of the stippled quilt, the stuffed and corded quilt, and the sampler of many different fancy motifs. Quilters never left their fancy designs floating in a large white space as we often do; they quilted closely spaced filler designs behind every feather and wreath. Among the most popular filler patterns were grids and diagonal lines. Nineteenth-century quilters especially liked to do double and triple line quilting with groups of lines ¼″ apart, and then an inch or so space before the next group of lines. They often used double lines to quilt feathers and leaves, outlining each image twice. The fashion for such fabulous quilting died out after the war. It's rare to find a stuffed or stippled quilt after 1865.

Most of the quilts shown in this book were quilted with far simpler quilting. In the twentieth century we do much of our simple quilting by stitching a line ¼″ inside the seam lines, emphasizing the patchwork pattern. Now we often quilt in the ditch, right in the seam line, to make our patchwork extra puffy.

During the 1840-1870 era quilters used a variety of simple quilting patterns that were utilitarian rather than fancy. They rarely did outline quilting around each piece. Quilting in the ditch was never used. We still use some of their utility designs like grids or patterns of parallel lines. They were just beginning to use the concentric patterns of curved lines we call Fans (the design is most common 1900-1950). One of their favorite patterns is one we've almost forgotten today, something still called elbow quilting in the South. The name must refer to the way the L-shaped design resembles your elbow.

The sketches of quilting drawn from period quilts feature several variations on the double and triple lines and methods for diagraming your top for different elbow quilting effects. The important thing in the elbow quilting is to ignore the patchwork.

Binding

Bindings have changed quite a bit over the past 150 years. During the Civil War era, quilters tended to add a narrow binding of a single strip of straight-grain fabric. Today, most quilters double their binding, make it wider, and often use bias grain binding. For an authentic look, try to make as narrow a binding as you can. The bindings on some of the elegant quilts from the era were approximately ⅜". To achieve this, start with a strip of straight grain fabric 1½" wide. Place the right side of the binding on the outer edge of the quilt top and stitch with a ¼" seam allowance. Fold the binding to the back of the quilt, turn it under ¼" and sew it down by hand. Don't forget, however, that quilters of the Civil War era were proud of their sewing machines and often finished off the binding by machine.

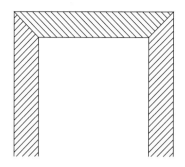

Another authentic look is a binding of cotton twill tape. It's difficult to find the right tape, but what you want is 100% cotton, white twill tape, about 1" wide. I usually dye mine with tea to give it the right antique look.

Inking

During the period discussed in this book, quiltmakers were quite likely to ink inscriptions on their quilts. About 1835 an inventor figured out a way to make an ink that was permanent on fabric, but not corrosive. Earlier inks, when permanent, would rot fabric, so most women marked their quilts with the cross-stitch they'd been taught as children. When the fabric-marking ink came on the market, it changed everything from the curriculum in girl's schools to the look of the quilt. After 1840 album quilts with elaborate inked signatures and drawings became the fashion. By the time the War was over, the tiny cross-stitch was almost forgotten.

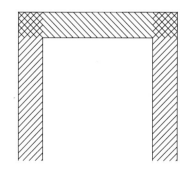

We see a revival of inking today, although we use tools other than quill pens and oak-gall ink. I have been using Pigma Micron® pens, especially the fine points marked #01. I occasionally use brown ink, but the nineteenth-century women used black, and their ink still looks black to us today 150 years later. I like the way the black shows up; the brown sometimes is just too soft.

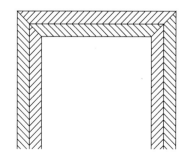

An album quilt is an excellent way to honor a group of people of the past. One can ink names of family members, soldiers in a regiment, or women in an organization. Civil War re-enactors might want to make blocks in the field and ask fellow re-enactors to sign the patches, inking a record of new and old friends.

Border Quilting

I trace most of my lettering. Some words I work out in an old-fashioned typeface using the word processing program on my computer. I then print out the text and trace it onto the fabric using my light box. If I am inking a signature I practice first on paper and then trace it.

I'm getting brave enough to ink the finished blocks, but you may want to begin by inking the pieces before they are assembled. One misspelled word can mean you have to start from scratch. If you're a beginner you might prefer the softer look of brown ink.

When you are copying mid-nineteenth-century handwriting (or making it up, as I often do) remember that they wrote in Spencerian style and we were taught to write in the Palmer style. In the late nineteenth century Palmer simplified the Spencerian hand which had odd conventions such as substituting a shape that looks like an "f" to us for a double "s." One of my treasures is an 1840-1850 autograph album. I often study its Spencerian script and the flourishes people added under their names before I do any inking. Look in the library for facsimile books that reproduce Spencerian handwriting if you want a real old-fashioned look to your inking.

Another book I refer to when inking quilts is a field guide to wild flowers that has hundreds of small floral images. A little sunflower under a Kansas signature, or a lily under a young woman's, is a wonderful flourish. For Civil War imagery I check the newspapers of the earlier days and today's Civil War magazines, which usually have interesting graphics. I have a file of eagles, shields, flags, and guns that I can use if I want to trace something patriotic either North or South. You can trace the examples below, as well as other examples sprinkled throughout this book, for your own inked details. You can enlarge them using a photocopy machine (See page 2 for photocopy permission.)

On the next few pages you'll find some poetry and songs you might want to ink on a Civil War quilt, and flourishes, and a few patriotic images.

What I Love
I love the man whose generous heart
Communes with the distressed
Whose head is open to relieve
The hopeless and oppressed.
(an abolitionist poem in Liberator)

The Bonnie Blue Flag (The Southern anthem)
By Harry McCarthy
We are a band of brothers and native to the soil
Fighting for the property we gained by honest toil.
And when our rights were threatened, the cry rose near and far
Hurrah for the Bonnie Blue Flag that bears a single star.
Hurrah! Hurrah! For Southern Rights Hurrah!
Hurrah for the Bonnie Blue Flag that bears a single star.

There was one of two things I had a right to
Liberty or Death
If I could not have one,
I would have the other
For no man should take me alive.
Harriet Tubman

The Battle Cry of Freedom
By George Frederick Root
The Union forever, hurrah! boys, hurrah,
Down with the Traitor, up with the star,
While we rally round the flag, boys, rally once again
Shouting the battle-cry of freedom.

Liberty and Union
Now and Forever
One and Inseparable
Daniel Webster

United States National Anthem
By William Ross Wallace
Then shout beside thine Oak, O North!
O South, wave answer with thy Palm!
And in our Union's heritage
Together sing the Nation's Psalm.

Dixie
By Albert Pike
Advance the flag of Dixie!
Hurrah! Hurrah!
For Dixie's Land we take our stand,
And live or die for Dixie

The Homespun Dress
By Carrie Bell Sinclair
Hurray! Hurrah!
For the Sunny South So Dear;
Three Cheers for the Homespun Dress
The Southern Ladies Wear.

"Mother! When around your child
You clasp your arm in love,
And when with grateful joy you raise
Your eyes to God above—
Think of the Negro-mother,
When her child is torn away—
Sold for a little slave—oh then,
For that poor mother pray!"

Away to the land of the North! for her star
Shall beacon thy course from its blue home afar–
W. H. Burleigh in Liberator, December 9, 1837

[Enlarge 366%]

Deliver me from the oppression of man.

INDEX

ABOUT THE AUTHOR

Barbara Brackman was born in New York City, but she has lived most of her life in Lawrence, Kansas, the site of much Civil War strife. She is well-known for her writing on quilt history. Her books *Clues in the Calico: A Guide to Identifying and Dating Antique Quilts*, *Encyclopedia of Pieced Patterns*, and *Encyclopedia of Appliqué Patterns* are standards for quilt and pattern identification. For many years she taught special education, but now she is a free-lance writer and museum curator. She has consulted for numerous regional and state quilt history projects and has guest curated exhibits for the Kansas Museum of History, the Autry Museum of Western Heritage, the Spencer Museum of Art, and the Knoxville Museum of Art, among others. Besides quilts and related textiles, she is also interested in women's history, folk art, and cowboy costume.

OTHER FINE BOOKS
FROM C&T PUBLISHING

Appliqué 12 Easy Ways! : Charming Quilts, Giftable Projects & Timeless Techniques, Elly Sienkiewicz

The Art of Classic Quiltmaking, Harriet Hargrave and Sharyn Craig

At Home with Patrick Lose: Colorful Quilted Projects, Patrick Lose

The Best of Baltimore Beauties, Elly Sienkiewicz

Color From the Heart: Seven Great Ways to Make Quilts with Colors You Love, Gai Perry

Curves in Motion: Quilt Designs & Techniques, Judy B. Dales

Exploring Machine Trapunto: New Dimensions, Hari Walner

Fabric Shopping with Alex Anderson, Seven Project to Help You: Make, Successful Choices, Build Your Confidence, Add to Your Fabric Stash, Alex Anderson

Fancy Appliqué: 12 Lessons to Enhance Your Skills, Elly Sienkiewicz

Fantastic Fabric Folding: Innovative Quilting Projects, Rebecca Wat

Freddy's House: Brilliant Color in Quilts, Freddy Moran

Free Stuff for Collectors on the Internet, Judy Heim and Gloria Hansen

Free Stuff for Crafty Kids on the Internet, Judy Heim and Gloria Hansen

Free Stuff for Gardeners on the Internet, Judy Heim and Gloria Hansen

Free Stuff for Quilters on the Internet, 2nd Ed. Judy Heim and Gloria Hansen

Free Stuff for Sewing Fanatics on the Internet, Judy Heim and Gloria Hansen

Free Stuff for Stitchers on the Internet, Judy Heim and Gloria Hansen

From Fiber to Fabric: The Essential Guide to Quiltmaking Textiles, Harriet Hargrave

Hand Quilting with Alex Anderson: Six Projects for Hand Quilters, Alex Anderson

Heirloom Machine Quilting, Third Edition, Harriet Hargrave

Jacobean Rhapsodies: Composing with 28 Appliqué Designs, Patricia B. Campbell and Mimi Ayars

Make Any Block Any Size, Joen Wolfrom

Mastering Machine Appliqué, Harriet Hargrave

Mastering Quilt Marking: Marking Tools & Techniques, Choosing Stencils, Matching Borders & Corners, Pepper Cory

The New England Quilt Museum Quilts: Featuring the Story of the Mill Girls. With Instructions for 5 Heirloom Quilts, Jennifer Gilbert

The Photo Transfer Handbook: Snap It, Print It, Stitch It!, Jean Ray Laury

Pieced Flowers, Ruth B. McDowell

Pieced Roman Shades: Turn Your Favorite Quilt Patterns into Window Hangings, Terrell Sundermann

Piecing: Expanding the Basics, Ruth B. McDowell

Quilt It for Kids; 11 Projects, Sports, Fantasy & Animal Themes, Quilts for Children of All Ages, Pam Bono

Quilts from Europe, Projects and Inspiration, Gül Laporte

Rotary Cutting with Alex Anderson: Tips, Techniques, and Projects, Alex Anderson

Rx for Quilters: Stitcher-Friendly Advice for Every Body, Susan Delaney Mech, M.D.

Scrap Quilts: The Art of Making Do, Roberta Horton

Shadow Quilts: Easy to Design Multiple Inage Quilts, Patricia Magaret and Donna Slusser

Simply Stars: Quilts that Sparkle, Alex Anderson

Skydyes: A Visual Guide to Fabric Painting, Mickey Lawler

Special Delivery Quilts, Patrick Lose

Start Quilting with Alex Anderson: Six Projects for First-Time Quilters, Alex Anderson

Through the Garden Gate: Quilters and Their Gardens, Jean and Valori Wells

Trapunto by Machine, Hari Walner

Travels with Peaky and Spike: Doreen Speckmann's Quilting Adventures, Doreen Speckmann

Wild Birds: Designs for Appliqué & Quilting, Carol Armstrong

Wildflowers: Designs for Appliqué & Quilting, Carol Armstrong

Women of Taste: A Collaboration Celebrating Quilt Artists and Chefs, Girls, Inc.

For more information write for a free catalog:
C&T Publishing, Inc.
P.O. Box 1456
Lafayette, CA 94549
(800) 284-1114
web: www.ctpub.com
e-mail: ctinfo@ctpub.com

For quilting supplies:
Cotton Patch Mail Order
3405 Hall Lane, Dept. CTB
Lafayette, CA 94549
(800) 835-4418
(925) 283-7883
web: www.quiltusa.com
e-mail: quiltusa@yahoo.com